The Slight EDGE

Secret to a $uccessful Life

The Slight EDGE

Secret to a $uccessful Life

Jeff Olson

momentum media
a division of VideoPlus, L.P.
Video *Plus*

This publication is designed to provide general information regarding the subject matter covered. However, laws and practices often vary from state to state and are subject to change. Because each factual situation is different, specific advice should be tailored to the particular circumstances. For this reason, the reader is advised to consult with his or her own advisor regarding their specific situation.

The author and publisher have taken reasonable precautions in the preparation of this book and believe the facts presented in the book are accurate as of the date it was written. However, neither the author nor the publisher assumes any responsibility for any errors or omissions. The author and publisher specifically disclaim any liability resulting from the use or application of the information contained in this book, and the information is not intended to serve as legal, financial or other professional advice related to individual situations.

Published by Momentum Media, a division of VideoPlus, L.P.

200 Swisher Road
Lake Dallas, Texas 75065
U.S.A.
Toll-free: 800.752.2030
Tel: 940.497.9700
www.VideoPlus.com
www.TapesandTools.com

VideoPlus is a registered trademark of VideoPlus, L.P.

Printed in the United States of America.

Designed by Momentum Media, a division of VideoPlus, L.P.

Library of Congress Control Number: 2005902199

ISBN 0-9672855-5-0

Contents

Acknowledgments

My thanks go to my mother, who has always believed in me; to Renée, my wife of eighteen years and friend for life, who has always stood by me; and to our precious daughter Amber, who is our proudest accomplishment. They have all been my own personal Slight Edge.

A special thanks to Jim Rohn, whose teachings have had a profound impact on me. It's often his wisdom you hear in these words.

To John David Mann, my coauthor, who brought his craft, passion, literary magic and good cheer to the project and made our book shine. To John Milton Fogg for his insights and his support, and for helping to get the ball rolling. To Stuart Johnson for helping this book, a dream of mine for many years, finally come to pass.

And to all who know that they have greatness deep inside them—and that it's just a Slight Edge away.

Introduction

The Shoeshine Woman

I arrived at the Phoenix airport about 6:30 in the morning. Having time before my plane left, I looked around to see if there was a place where I could get my shoes shined. There was hardly anybody in the airport at that time of the morning. I strolled around.

Before long, I found a shoeshine stand. It was open; a woman in her mid to late forties sat in one of the customer chairs, absorbed in a paperback book. She was dressed in black stretch pants, a black apron and a white shirt. Seemed like a nice, solid person.

I walked over to her stand.

The woman greeted me warmly. She was friendly and happy—*not always an easy way to be before the sun comes up,* I thought. She got up, set down her book, first carefully folding over the corner of the page she'd been reading, then took up the tools of her trade and pleasantly ushered me into the chair.

Her stand was located right next to a service door through which a constant stream of maintenance men and janitors came and went. *Got to be at work by seven,* I guessed. As they passed by our shoeshine stand, every one of these men stopped and exchanged greetings with the woman. She knew them all by name and they knew hers, too. It was clear they were all friends.

She went to work on my shoes, and we started talking.

Her daughter, she told me, had just won a cheerleading contest. Boy was she proud of her! The girl was hoping to go to a cheerleading camp in Dallas. "Tell you the truth," she confided, her voice dropping a bit, "I don't know how in the world I'm going to find the money to buy her the uniform and plane ticket, let alone the camp tuition."

In just the few minutes that I sat with this woman, I learned a good deal about her life—and about her. She loved her family, and for that matter, liked people in general. She made friends easily and was a natural-born communicator. It was also clear that she enjoyed her work.

And it's a good thing she does, I thought—because she'd been there, shining shoes in that same spot, for more than five years.

I couldn't help but wonder what this woman's life would be like if she had taken a different path five years earlier. She was well spoken, carried herself well, was friendly and affable.

With different clothes and a little attention to her hair, she could easily pass for a successful businessperson.

I noticed the book she'd been reading. It was a popular novel, something to pass the time, to survive the stretches of occupational boredom by living vicariously in someone else's imagined romance. There was a little heap of them sitting dog-eared by the wall.

What if, instead of spending ten or fifteen minutes here and there, tucked in between customers, sinking into the pages of those forgettable novels, she had spent the last five years reading books that were genuinely life changing? What if that little stack of books included Napoleon Hill's Think and Grow Rich, *Stephen Covey's* The 7 Habits of Highly Effective People, *or David Bach's* Smart Women Finish Rich? *Where would she be today?*

The shoeshine woman was a hard worker. Good with people. She knew how to read and clearly enjoyed doing so. She was a superb communicator. She obviously had the talent, personality and basic life skills to accomplish a lot more than just living off tips from shining the shoes of people who could afford to buy their kids new uniforms and tickets to Dallas.

But she was spending her life building other people's dreams—not her own.

Your income tends to equal the average of the incomes of your five best friends, I mused. What if she had spent time around people with significantly higher incomes than her own? What if, instead of hanging out only with her colleagues here in the airport, she had cultivated a different group of friends? What if she'd been associating with powerful people, successful people, mentors, movers, shakers, leaders? She could easily have done this—she's a terrific conversationalist. If she had, where would she be today?

I'm not making a value judgment on modest incomes or simple occupations. There are people who work the humblest of jobs yet live lives rich in relationships and joy, just as there are extremely wealthy people who are also extremely unhappy. And I'm not criticizing popular novels. But it was clear that this woman was struggling, and as we sat there talking, I'd have bet anything that she wanted more out of life.

It was clear that she wanted to give her daughter the uniform and the Dallas trip, things she couldn't afford in the life she was living. And it was clear that it was so much on her mind, she'd confided her worries to a complete stranger within five minutes of meeting him.

She wanted more, it was plain to see. Why didn't she have it?

She's industrious, motivated and smart. She reads. She listens. She's sharp. Where would she be today if she'd set foot on a different path a year ago? Five years ago? You can bet she wouldn't be shining my shoes. Managing a chain of shoeshine stands is more like it. Would she be having any trouble sending her daughter to Dallas? I bet she'd be sponsoring the entire team—and going with them, too!

While this woman with the wonderful personality continued shining my shoes, I was watching her in my mind's eye, seeing her on a plane to Texas surrounded by giggling, excited, happy teenagers, seeing her being successful in so many different ways, in so many areas, making such a difference in her own life and the lives of so many others, if only ... what? What was missing?

Feelings welled up in me, a mix of frustration and sadness. I felt for a moment as if I were going to cry, and I wondered, *Why are you so moved by all of this? You've seen this before a hundred times—why are you so affected by it all?*

One reason, I knew, was that it reminded me of another character I'd observed before—nice, like the shoeshine woman, a good person ... just not succeeding in life.

The Beach Bum

I was born and raised in Albuquerque, New Mexico. My dad died when I was ten; I remember being handed the flag from his casket. My mom held everything together; she was a great, loving mom. But it was still a rough way to grow up: a fatherless, blond-headed kid in a Hispanic neighborhood, who didn't fit in. I really didn't know what to do with it all, so I turned my energy into mischief and misbehavior: I blamed everything and everyone.

In third grade, my teachers informed me that I had a low I.Q. I quickly gained a reputation for mischief and trouble making. While my mom worked her way through the years, I struggled my way through school. By age nineteen, it was clear to anyone who knew me that I didn't have much of a future.

I begged my way into the University of New Mexico. At college, I built on my previous academic career and succeeded in taking my C average to a D average. I did learn one thing, though: I learned that when spring break came, all the students went to Daytona Beach for a week. I thought I could do one better—I quit school and moved there.

At Daytona Beach, I pursued my first profession: I became a beach bum. I lifted weights and chased girls. I let my hair grow long and curly. People started calling me "Gorgeous George" after the wrestler.

I got a job at the Orlando Country Club cutting the grass on the golf course. One day, as I was cutting the greens in the hot Florida sun, I paused to watch the wealthy club members playing golf on the grass I had cut. As I watched them hum to and fro in their zippy golf carts, in dapper fine golf outfits, with their classy golf bags filled with expensive golf clubs, I felt a burning question simmer up inside.

Why is it that they're over there riding in carts, and I'm over here working?

I don't get it. Why are they putting and I'm cutting? How come they're driving nice cars, wearing nice clothes and having a great time—and I'm here sweating in cut-offs with a beat-up '64 Dodge Dart that overheats before it gets off the driveway? I don't get it! I'm as good as these people are. How do they get to have it ten times better than me? ARE they ten times better than me? Are they ten times smarter? Or do they work ten times harder? Or ... ?

If Only ...

"You're lookin' good, sir, lookin' good."

The shoeshine woman was grinning at me. *Another customer lost in his early morning thoughts. And another job well done.* I looked down: I could see my reflection in my shoes.

Indeed I am. Lookin' good ... thank you. Thanks very much.

I paid her, gave her as big a tip as I could without (I hoped) having her feel I was being patronizing, and walked away with clean shoes and a heavy heart.

It had taken many years, but I was fortunate enough to have found my way out of my beach bum career. I was no longer cutting the greens of other people's leisurely pursuits. I had found my way to a good life.

She was right; for me, things were *lookin' good, sir, lookin' good.*

But why the beach bum and not the shoeshine woman?

While my shoes had been getting a shine, the airport had grown busier. I now walked through a growing throng of travelers as I worked my way toward my gate. I noticed all the faces filing past me. Hardly anyone was smiling. Most of my fellow travelers were trudging with their heads bowed down. I saw bored expressions. Vacant. *Porch light's on, dog's barking, but nobody's home.*

Everybody looked so tired. Failing is exhausting.

I heard angry words.

I stopped for a cup of coffee and heard a young couple arguing with each other. A burly man scolded his young son to the point of tears. A heavy woman complained about the service, then the prices, then her food, and then started back in on the service again. The other people in line nodded their heads. A few joined her in a chorus of negativity.

Why is everyone so ... down? Everything these people need to know to change their lives for the better is already available. All the information they could possibly need to put them on a path of extraordinary success and fulfillment is out there, in books and tapes, videos and workshops. There are people to help them—rich, living resources to guide them, be their mentors, teachers, coaches and allies.

I knew that the difference between who they were and who they could be wasn't based on any lack of good information. It was all already available.

But why, if the information is all there, all the resources are there, and these people really do want to succeed, then why aren't they doing it?

I looked around the airport as the early morning rush hour swelled its ranks of busy, hurrying, scowling, unhappy people shambling past with no spark in their faces, no bounce in their step. I wished I could somehow address them all, that I could touch all their lives with my silent soliloquy.

The problem, I shouted out in my head, *is that you don't have a way to process the information. There's no framework in place for you to take in all the extraordinary insight that's out there and put it to work in your life.*

If only you were aware of the Slight Edge. If only you knew what it was doing in your life and how easy it is to have the Slight Edge working for you—instead of against you.

If only you were making the right choices, doing those simple, little disciplines that would change your life for the better forever ... where would you be five years from today?

If only you learned to recognize the Slight Edge ...

If only ...

But it was only in my head. Not a soul heard my words ... nobody, that is, but me.

That day, on the plane, I started writing this book.

The Slight Edge is not just more good information. It's not another self-help success book packed with some revolutionary "new best way" of doing things. You don't need that. Nobody needs that. All the "new and better" information is already available and has been for years.

This book is designed to help you use that information.

This book is what I wish will help you take whatever information you want, whatever how-to's or strategies or goals or aspirations, and turn them into the life you want. This book is what I wish I could have put into that sweet and sad shoeshine woman's hands.

I have since been back to that airport. In fact, I have been back through there many, many times. I have looked for the shoeshine woman, but she is no longer there. I don't know where she is or what has happened in her life. But I do know this: she is not alone. There are millions upon millions of people, everywhere I go, everywhere I look, whose lives are not all that they wish, not all that they yearn for. Not even close.

And yet they could be.

So I dedicate this book to that shoeshine woman, to her daughter, to her daughter's cheerleading team ... and to everyone else in the world who wants more.

I dedicate this book to *you*.

Three Stories

The Water Hyacinth

The water hyacinth is a beautiful, delicate-looking little plant. Prized as an ornament, it sports six-petaled flowers ranging from a lovely purplish blue, to lavender, to pink. You can find it floating on the surface of ponds in warm climates around the world.

The water hyacinth is also one of the most productive plants on earth; its reproductive rate astonishes botanists and ecologists. Although a single plant can produce as many as 5,000 seeds, the method it prefers for colonizing a new area is to grow by doubling itself, sending out short runner stems that become "daughter plants."

If a pond's surface is fairly still and undisturbed, the water hyacinth may cover the entire pond in thirty days.

On the first day, you won't even notice it. In fact, for the first few weeks you will have to search very hard to find it. On day 15, it will cover perhaps a single square foot of the pond's surface ... a barely significant dollop of color dotting the expanse of placid green.

On the twentieth day (two-thirds of the way to the end of the month), you may happen to notice a dense little patch of floating foliage, about the size of a small mattress. You would be easily forgiven if you mistook it for a boy's inflatable life raft, left behind during a family picnic.

On day 29, one-half of the pond's surface will be open water.

On the thirtieth day, the entire pond will be covered by a blanket of water hyacinth.

You will not see any water at all.

Two Frogs

One night, two frogs left the safety of their swamp and ventured into a nearby farm to explore. They soon found themselves in a dairy. Hopping and jumping around (frogs will be frogs, after all), they jumped into a milk pail half full of cream.

At first, they were both thrilled. They had never tasted anything so delicious! They drank and drank. Soon (after some contented frog belches followed by much giggling) they were both full-bellied and getting just a bit sleepy. "Time to get out of here and head back to the swamp for some shut-eye," burped the first frog.

But there was a problem. They'd had no trouble hopping in ... but how to hop out? The inside of the pail was too slippery to climb, and there was nothing on which they could place their feet for traction to get up a good hopping distance ... or any hopping distance at all.

The awful reality dawned on them: they were trapped.

Frantic, they began to thrash about, their little frog feet scrabbling for a foothold on the elusive, slippery curve of the pail's edge.

Finally, the second frog cried out, "It's no use! We're doomed, my brother! Let us save what dignity we have left and die here like frogs, with our eyes facing our homeland!"

The first frog cried out to stop him. "No! We should never give up! When we were tadpoles, which of us would ever have dreamed that some day we would emerge from the water and hop about on land? Swim on, and pray for a miracle!"

The second frog eyed his brother sadly and said, "There are no miracles in the life of a frog, brother. Farewell." And so saying, he turned his face in the direction of the swamp, gave a sigh, and slowly sank out of sight.

But the first frog refused to give up.

He continued to swim. He swam and he swam in ridiculous, pointless, useless, futile circles, hoping against hope for a miracle. Fired by adrenaline, he paddled mightily ... yet his brother's dying words clutched at his thoughts, even more insidious than the growing fatigue that tugged at his weakening muscles. *Was my brother right?*, he thought desperately. *Am I a fool? Are there no miracles in the life of a frog?*

Finally, he could swim no more ... and with a great cry of anguish, he stopped paddling and let go, ready at last to face his fate like a frog.

But something odd then happened ... or rather, *didn't* happen. He didn't sink. He just sat exactly where he was. Ever so tentatively, he stretched out a foot ... and felt it touch something solid.

He heaved a big sigh, both sad and grateful, said a silent farewell to his drowned brother, then scrambled up on top of the big lump of butter he had just finished churning ...

... and hopped out of the pail and off to the swamp, alone but alive.

The Choice

A wealthy man nearing the end of his days summoned his twin sons to his bedside. Before he died, he told them, he wanted to pass on to them the opportunity to experience the richness of life that he had enjoyed for his many years on earth.

"If I could do so, I would give you both the world," he told his boys, "but this is not possible, for even I do not own the entire world and everything in it. But there are three treasures I have had the good fortune to experience in my life, and it is my fondest wish, my dying wish, that you would both have these three treasures.

"The first gift is easy to give, and never runs out. I have been giving it to you both since you were born, and die in peace knowing that you both already have it in abundance.

"The second gift is easy to give, but not always easy to have. For some, it never runs out, while for others, it constantly runs out. This gift I give you now, but whether or not you keep it will be up to you.

"The third gift is impossible to give, but can only be gained. I have been showing it to you both your entire lives, but cannot say whether or not you have gained it. This gift I cannot give you, but I can give you an opportunity to see it one last time before I die."

The boys both wept to hear their father speak of his approaching death, but he smiled and bade them hush with a wave of his hand.

"I see your grief, but in that grief you may be happy, for it is evidence of the first gift, which you have in abundance. Do you know what the first gift is?"

The two boys dried their tears and furrowed their brows in deep thought. *Easy to give, and it never runs out …*

Suddenly the first boy clapped his hands and said, "Love! The first gift is love!" The father smiled. The boy was right. "And the second gift?" he asked them.

They again became quiet with thought. *Easy to give, but not always easy to have …*

The second boy looked up with a start. "Money? Is the second gift money?" It was indeed. *For some, it never runs out, while for others, it constantly runs out.*

"And the third?"

Impossible to give, can only be gained …

This time both boys remained buried in thought. Neither could come up with an answer.

The father smiled again, a little sadly this time. He lifted a beautiful lacquer box from the bedside table onto his lap, opened it and looked inside.

"I offer you both a choice."

He beckoned the boys to move closer.

"One month from today, you both will turn twenty-one. I will no longer be with you, for my life has run its course. On that day, thirty-one days from now, I have instructed my most trusted advisor to execute a document that will bequeath my home, my treasury, my estate—all that I possess—to the good people of this land, who have treated me with kindness all these years. This place, which has been our home together for these twenty-one years, will become a public trust. I will be well on my way to the next world, and the two of you will set off to make your way in this one.

"Yet I do not wish you to set foot on this journey empty-handed. My last gift to you, on the day of your departure, will be a purse to finance your adventures.

"What goes into each purse is your choice."

He reached both hands inside the box, and then held them

out to the boys. In one hand, he held a sheaf of one thousand crisp, new $1,000 bills. One million dollars. Cash. In the other hand, he held a shiny new copper penny.

"If you take the million in cash, you may take it with you or leave it in your purse for safe-keeping until the day of your journey; your purse will be held by my treasury director.

"If you take the penny, you may also take it with you or leave it in your purse. However, if you choose the penny, my treasury director has instructions to double the contents of your purse every day."

He took out another lacquer box, identical to the first, opened it, and took out another stack of $1,000 bills and another penny.

"Here is one million; here is one penny. You each have the same choice to make. Whatever you do not take, I will return to my treasury to add to my estate.

"Now, go, rest, and think. Tomorrow morning, come back and tell me your choice."

All night, the first boy lay in bed thinking, *What should I do? Which should I take? What is the lesson?* The second boy lay awake, too, but he asked himself different questions. He had made his decision before his father had finished the sentence. Now he was making careful plans for what to do for the next thirty-one days.

When morning came, the second boy sprang into action. After securing the million in cash from his father, he hired a sharp consultant and a manager to help him execute his carefully wrought plan. They rented out a hotel suite, in which they conducted exhaustive, back-to-back interviews for the next six days. By week's end, they had hired a staff of the finest financial advisors in the land.

The boy's new crackerjack money-man team spent the second week in intensive, round-the-clock brainstorming sessions, drafting proposal after proposal, seeking the smartest, most cost-effective investment and leveraging strategies, both long-term and short-term, to help the wealthy man's son turn his million into a genuine fortune.

By week three, the best plans had been selected, winnowed, examined, combed, explored, game-theoried, road-tested, computer-simulated and dissected. With all their i's dotted and all their t's crossed, the boy's advisors were locked and loaded and ready to rumble. Off they went, into the battlefields of commerce and speculation. The boy spent the next few days keeping in close contact with his far-flung financial team by telephone; but by mid-week, it seemed clear that things were well in hand and he was not needed. He decided to pay a visit to his brother, whom he had not seen since breakfast on the morning after that long and sleepless night.

When he arrived at their home, he was shocked to hear his brother's account of the past few weeks.

After that excited breakfast, the first boy had also paid a visit to his father, but without explaining why, he announced that he had made the second choice. He had taken the penny, left it in the purse, then returned to his room and began reading from one of his favorite books.

The second day, he visited again, and was allowed to peek into the purse: the shiny new penny had been joined by a companion. On the third day, he found four pennies. On the fourth, there were eight, and on the fifth, sixteen, then thirty-two.

By the end of the week, just as his brother's ace financial team was assembling in the beautiful hotel suite for the first time, he had amassed a nest egg of sixty-four cents. By the end of week two—with nearly half the month gone—his piles of pennies had swelled to just shy of ninety dollars ... $81.92, to be exact.

On the day his brother's financial team hit the streets and went out into the world ready to turn his million into billions, his purse had not yet accumulated a hundred dollars—he would not have been able to purchase even a decent dinner for two at the fine hotel where his brother's suite had been humming with action for two weeks.

Now, a few days into the third week, the purse's contents had grown a bit more: he now had a sum of $655 ("and thirty-six cents," he proudly pointed out)—easily enough to sustain him on the road for a full week.

"But you poor sap!" his brother cried on hearing his story. "I can't believe you went for the penny! It's not too late—visit our father, see if he will relent and give you your own million. Or if he insists in prorating the amount, then even just half the million—

it's better than scrabbling by on a few paltry hundred! And if he refuses, you've got to let me help ... I can't stand the idea of you venturing out into the world with scarcely enough to feed yourself for a week!"

But the brother seemed unperturbed and wouldn't hear of it.

Later that week, the wealthy man called his sons to him one more time and spent several hours with them, sharing memories and telling stories. They both left him in good spirits (though the second boy was secretly very worried about his brother's prospects).

That night, the old man died peacefully in his sleep.

Toward the end of week four, the second boy's top advisors brought him some worrisome news. The markets, it seemed, had gone a bit soft. Taken a bit of a tumble, actually. The team had acted quickly and salvaged what they could, but their earlier rosy projections would most certainly need to be revised downward.

The boy thanked them for their vigilance, and waited, fretting and anxious.

At the close of the week, the team brought mixed news. Some investments had performed quite well, others had suffered. All in all, the boy had made a modest gain: starting with his one million in cash, his team had succeeded in parleying that into nearly one and a half million. Unfortunately, his expenses, including their commissions, tax, bills for the hotel suite, broker fees and the rest, came to just over half a million.

The boy had ended the month with just a bit less than he started!

In a panic, he rushed to see his brother, to see how he had fared with his $655 (and thirty-six cents)—only to receive yet another shock. On day 28, his brother's purse of pennies had passed the million-dollar mark. On day 29, the two-and-a-half-million mark. Yesterday, on day 30, it had doubled to *more than five million!*

The boy who chose the penny had discovered the extraordinary power that some have called "the eighth wonder of the world"—the remarkable creative force of *compound interest.*

And today, the boy who chose the penny was worth more than *ten* million dollars—$10,737,418 ... and twenty-four cents.

A Question

Two boys. Two frogs. Two powerful choices. Riches or poverty. Life or death.

You are making those same choices, every day, every hour, and the choices you make are spreading out through your life, just like the water hyacinth. You may not see the results today, or tomorrow, or even next year. In fact, by the time you do finally see the results, the process will probably be so far along that the surface of the pond will be completely covered.

The question is, covered with what?

When the wealthy man spoke to his sons, the second boy thought he was offering them a choice of *which money* to take. But the first boy listened more carefully. He remembered that money was only the second gift. He understood that the choice was not whether to take the penny or the sheaf of bills—the choice was whether or not to take the third gift.

Wisdom.

The lesson was not about money: it was about wisdom. It was a lesson about compound interest, leverage, geometric progression and growth. It was a lesson about the Slight Edge.

The choice the wealthy man offered his two sons is the same choice the world offers you, every day, every hour: sickness or health; sinking poverty or abundant wealth; deepening loneliness and alienation or a rich and growing circle of friends.

The Slight Edge will be your guide to the wealthy man's third gift; it will help you learn habits of thought and action that will allow you to choose the penny doubled, every time. It will keep you paddling until your cream becomes butter. It will give you the power to choose what to plant in your life, so that you will end up completely blanketing the surface of the pond with the blossoms of your choice.

PART ONE

The Slight Edge

CHAPTER 1

The Slight Edge

The law of nature is, Do the thing, and you shall have the power:
but they who do not the thing have not the power.

— Ralph Waldo Emerson, *Compensation*
(Essays: First Series, 1841)

Take two seemingly similar people and give them both the exact
same opportunity. One takes it and has remarkable success, the
other doesn't. One wins, the other does not.

Why?

During my years in business, I've worked with several thousand people from every imaginable walk of life. They have all had
the exact same opportunity. Several dozen of these people have
become millionaires. Many more have earned a good, solid living.
But the great majority of them, faced with exactly the same opportunities, have gone nowhere.

Why? It's not a matter of luck. Nor is it timing, nor fate. It's
not a matter of intelligence, skill or talent, either.

During these same years, I've gone to the very top with many
different companies, with different product lines, in different
countries and different languages (which I don't speak). In case
you're worried that I'm bragging, let me put your mind at ease:
there was absolutely nothing brilliant about what I did. Actually,
it was quite the opposite. In every case, I did the exact same thing
every time, using ridiculously simple strategies made up of ridiculously simple lists of ridiculously simple actions.

And in case you're now thinking that I'm exaggerating, that those are statements of false modesty, let me put your mind at ease about that, too. The strategies I used—none of them invented or devised by me, incidentally—are so simple that if you and I sat down together in a room for twenty minutes, I could show you exactly what I did to create four different, separate, independent multimillion-dollar organizations—and teach you how to do the exact same thing. In twenty minutes.

And chances are, it wouldn't work for you.

Why not? Because *how* to do it is not the issue. Because, if we don't change the way you think, then you'll have rearranged what I said by the time you leave the room. You'll have reinvented it by the time you go to bed that night and in the morning, you won't even recognize it as the same information.

People everywhere are clamoring for the formula, the secret, the path to improve their lives. *Tell me how you did this, so I can do it, too. Give me the definitive plan. Tell me how to be healthy. Tell me how to be rich. Tell me how to be happy. Tell me, tell me, tell me ...* and there's more good, solid how-to information available today about all those things and more than there's ever been in history. But that's not how it works. If you're one of the millions looking for cookie-cutter answers to the great questions in life, you can call off the search right now! *How to do it* is not the issue.

If "how to do it" were the answer, it'd be done. If access to the right information were the answer, we'd all be rich, healthy, happy and fulfilled. And most of us are none of those things.

Why not? Because the answer is only the answer—it isn't actually doing the thing. It isn't *applying* the answer, *living* the answer. It's only information.

It's not that how-to books are not valuable; there are some wonderful ones I'll even recommend to you at the end of this book. It's just that another how-to book is not what you need. It's not what any of us need. We already have enough of those— maybe more than enough. Because what you need to transform your life is not more information.

Besides, we're all so different; my how-to may not be yours. It may work for me, but it may not be the how-to that works for you. As much as we'd all love to quantify a precise, specific, paint-by-the-numbers approach to life, love and happiness, we are out of luck in that department because there is no universal, one-size-fits-all method to anything. However ...

The Secret Ingredient

However, there is a secret ingredient.

There is a secret that, once you know it, will cause you to find those answers, apply them, live them, and achieve those results you want.

The secret ingredient is your philosophy. The secret is to change the way you think. Once you do, then you will take the steps you need to take, to lead you to the how-to's you need. If you don't change your thinking, no amount of how-to's will offer a real solution.

This isn't about self-hypnosis, or about conjuring up the impossible through sheer positive thinking, or any other kind of hocus-pocus. And I'm not talking about some complex, elaborate or heady system of ideas. And—although I'll completely understand if you find the last part of this sentence truly difficult to believe—*what I'm talking about is not difficult to do.*

It simply means changing your thinking. Your philosophy.

The reason diets and other how-to's don't work for most people is the same reason most how-to books and courses don't work for most people. It isn't that the actions are wrong. It's that people don't keep doing them.

Focusing on the actions (the what-to-do's and the how-to-do-it's) is not enough, because it's the *attitude behind the actions* that keep those actions in place.

Aha! It's attitudes! So, what I need is an attitude adjustment ...

No, that won't do it either. Focusing on attitudes isn't any more effective than focusing on actions, because attitudes are fickle. Your emotions change. You can't dictate how you feel. No matter how much you may tell yourself to feel positive about this how-to step or that how-to step, what if you just don't? Today, you're excited about getting fit. You feel like doing your twenty minutes on the treadmill. Great! But what if tomorrow you just don't feel like doing it?

To find the path to success, you have to back up one more step. It's the understanding behind the attitudes that are behind the actions.

It's the philosophy. That's the secret ingredient. Your philosophy is what you know, how you hold it, and how it affects what you do. That's what this book is about.

Yes, you have to know the winning how-to actions, and you have to possess the winning attitudes—but what generates all that and keeps it all in place is your philosophy.

A positive philosophy turns into a positive attitude, which turns into positive actions, which turns into positive results, which turns into a positive lifestyle.

A negative philosophy turns into a negative attitude, which turns into negative actions, which turns into negative results, which turns into a negative lifestyle.

Life Wisdom

What do I mean by philosophy? Not something lofty or abstract; not something you need to go to graduate school or learn Greek to understand. I mean something so simple, so basic, a six-year-old child can understand it.

Here is an example.

Do the thing, and you shall have the power.
                    — Ralph Waldo Emerson, *Compensation*

Profoundly simple and just as powerful. The sort of wisdom you can actually apply in everyday life. Nike simplified it for the MTV generation ("Just do it"), but I like the Emerson version better, and we'll be using it a good deal later on when we talk about applying the Slight Edge to your life.

There are two prevalent types of attitudes: entitled and value-driven. A value-driven attitude says, "What can I do to help you?" An entitled attitude says, "What have you done for me lately?" An entitled attitude says, "Pay me more, and then maybe I'll work harder." A value-driven attitude says, "I'll work harder, and then I expect you'll pay me more."

Which of these attitudes is driven by Emerson's philosophy, "Do the thing and you'll have the power"?

Your philosophy is *what you know, how you hold what you know, and how it affects what you do.* You can look at anyone's actions and trace back, through the attitudes behind those actions, to their source: the philosophy behind the attitudes. Show me what a man does, and I'll show you what his philosophy is.

Here's another example of a life philosophy:

> The formula for success is quite simple: double your rate of failure.
>
> — Thomas J. Watson, Sr. (founder of IBM)

We are not taught that the key to success is to "double your rate of failure." On the contrary, we're taught to avoid failure like the plague. "Failure is not an option!" Really? It had better be an option! It had better be, because whether or not you consider it an option, it's going to happen.

If you go through life with the philosophy that "failure is not an option," then you'll never have any good opportunities to learn. (Which won't really matter anyway, because if failing is not an option, chances are you won't even try in the first place!)

If Babe Ruth had had the philosophy, "Failure is not an option," then you and I would have never heard of him. Why? Because not only did Babe Ruth set a world record for home runs, he also led the league in strikeouts.

Abraham Lincoln had an extraordinary record of lost elections and public-office failures over the course of his career. For the ungainly lawyer from Illinois, failure was not only an option, it was practically his specialty. If it hadn't been, he would never have made it to the White House.

And it's hard to imagine just what our lives would be like today if Thomas Edison had subscribed to the "Failure is not an option" philosophy. In his efforts to find a stable filament to make his electric light bulb invention work, he tried out thousands of different versions and every single one failed. His comment: "I have not failed. I've simply discovered ten thousand ways that don't work."

Successful people *fail* their way to the top!

The Slight Edge Philosophy

Your philosophy is your view of life, something beyond feelings and attitudes. Your philosophy drives your attitudes and feelings, which drive your actions.

By and large, people are looking in the wrong places. They are looking for a breakthrough, looking for that amazing "quantum leap"—the philosophy of the craps table and roulette wheel. I don't believe they'll ever find it. I've had colossal failures, and I've had remarkable successes, and my experience is, neither one happens in quantum leaps. They happen through the Slight Edge.

The purpose of this book is to have you understand the Slight Edge philosophy, to make it part of how you see the world and how you live your life every day. To understand patience; to understand that little steps, compounded, do make a difference. That the things you do every single day, the things that don't look dramatic, that don't even look like they matter, do matter. That they not only make a difference—they make *all* the difference.

Throughout this book, if you look carefully, you'll find at least a dozen statements (and if you look really closely, many dozens!) that embody this philosophy, statements such as "Do the thing, and you shall have the power." Here are a few more examples that you'll come across in the following pages:

Success is the progressive realization of a worthy ideal.

Successful people do what unsuccessful people are not willing to do.

There is a natural progression to everything in life: plant, cultivate, harvest.

Here's a suggestion that can maximize how much you get out of this book—that is, not only reading it, but also absorbing it and applying it in your life: every time you come to a fundamental statement of philosophy, highlight it. Then go back regularly and read through just those highlighted sections: your own personal guide to the Slight Edge philosophy.

The Slight Edge is also the philosophy embodied in the three stories you read in the beginning of this book. It is understanding the tremendous potential of something as seemingly insignificant as a penny. It is knowing how to recognize and harness the power of the water hyacinth. It's having faith in the process of simple, positive actions repeated over time, the faith that miracles do happen—if you know when to trust the process and keep churning the cream.

Just Add Life and Stir ...

The Slight Edge is the missing ingredient you need for all the self-help books, how-to's and life guides to work.

If you don't grasp the truth of the Slight Edge, then no matter what health books you read, you're not going to be willing to do the little things that lead you to a healthy life. No matter what you learn, no matter how many books you read, tapes and CDs you listen to, or seminars you attend, if you don't absorb this philosophy of simple steps and their compounded effect over time, you won't successfully apply those things you learn to create the results you want.

The Slight Edge is the book you need to read before you read the health book, the sales book, the investment book, the positive attitude book. The Slight Edge is the book you need to read, highlight and reread along with your fitness class, your career planning, your continuing education and pursuit of new skills. The book to keep with you as you set out to grow and pursue greater accomplishment, achievement and fulfillment in any area of your life.

The Slight Edge will prepare you to be able to absorb all that other information, guidance and education from all those other books, classes, situations and experiences.

If the thing you want to accomplish—your financial goals, life skills, fitness and better health, better relationships, greater knowledge, professional accomplishment ... whatever it is—if that's the meal you want to eat, *The Slight Edge* is the enzyme that will enable you to digest it. If your life pursuits are programs you want to run, *The Slight Edge* is the operating system you need to run them. Whatever pictures you want to create in your life, *The Slight Edge* is the brush and the paint.

What are you after? What do you want more of in your life? Better health, a feeling of vitality and renewed vigor, to feel the kind of energy you used to feel when you were younger? Richer and more satisfying relationships with your family, friends and colleagues? A happier marriage? Financial freedom and long-term financial security? A greater sense of meaning in your life? More involvement in your spiritual life, in making contributions to your community, or to others less fortunate, at home or around the world? Is there a new skill, a new sport, a new pursuit, a new career you want to master? A new place you want to move to, places to travel, a different home to live in?

Whatever it is, I want you to have it, and I know you can. That is my passionate belief—and I've seen it happen too many times to doubt it. But you need a place to start. *The Slight Edge* is that starting point. It's the first ingredient.

After that, just add life and stir.

CHAPTER 2

The Secret of Easy Things

'Tis a gift to be simple, 'tis a gift to be free,
'Tis a gift to come down where you ought to be,
And when we find ourselves in the place just right
'Twill be in the valley of love and delight.

— traditional Shaker hymn

Have you ever met a really successful person? You know whom I mean: that woman with the easy, engaging smile, the one who makes you feel instantly at ease, even as you stand in awe of her accomplishments. The guy who's always dressed for success, who looks great even when he isn't trying, and somehow makes you feel better about yourself just being in his presence. People who not only are successful, but also seem to breathe success and fill the space around them with it.

They live in beautiful homes, travel to exciting places, fly first class. Are surrounded by people who love them and admire them. Are appreciated, respected and recognized. Happy, healthy, creative and fulfilled. Winners in the game of life.

Why do some families have such great relationships, such warmth and fun and caring closeness, while others are perennially angry with each other, so distrustful and distant they might as well live on different planets? Why are some people positive and upbeat while others are miserably negative, constantly complaining and criticizing?

Why is it some people never seem to manage the time to stay in shape, while others run a few miles each day even though their lives are just as busy? Why are some people digging deeper and deeper into debt, while others just keep earning more money?

Why is it that some people seem to make dream after dream come true, while others spend their lives building someone else's dream? Why are some people successful, and some people failures?

What's the difference—really?

What Do Successful People Do?

You've probably read and heard lots of statistics. Happy versus unhappy marriages, health versus illness, how many retirees barely survive on fixed incomes versus how many reach their golden years in comfort and security. There are a hundred and one ways to measure it, but if you simply look around you, you can see it: most of us aren't making it.

My observation is that about one person in twenty is achieving a significant measure of his or her goals in life: financial, professional, personal, marital, spiritual, in terms of health, in whatever terms you want to look at. Ninety-five percent are either failing or falling short.

What are the five percent doing that the ninety-five percent are not?

There is only one difference. It is not heredity, education, looks, talent or inheritance. It is not "preparedness meeting opportunity," and it's not chance, either. There is only one difference, and that difference is the Slight Edge.

If you will learn to understand and apply the Slight Edge, I will guarantee you that in time—and chances are, less time than you would imagine—you will have what you want. You will be among the five percent. You will be successful. *And you will achieve those aims, goals and dreams by doing simple things.*

A bold claim, I know, and I make it only because I know it's true—I've seen it too many times to doubt it. If you learn to understand and apply the Slight Edge, your life will become filled with hundreds of thousands of small, seemingly insignificant actions—all of them easy to do, none of them mysterious, complex or difficult. And those actions will create your success.

That's what successful people do: simple things that are easy to do.

Simple Things

"Wait a minute. How are these simple, everyday actions supposed to create all this wonderful happiness, health and success for me, if they're all easy to do—if anyone could do them? If these are things anyone can do, why are only five percent successful?"

Excellent question. Because they're all also easy *not to do*—and while anyone *could* do them, most *won't*.

Fundamentally, we all take pretty much the same actions every day. We eat, sleep, think, feel, talk and listen. We have relationships and friendships. We each have twenty-four hours a day, 8,760 hours a year, and we each fill these hours one way or the other with a sequence of little tasks and actions, any one of which is seemingly insignificant.

Gold medal marathon runners eat and sleep. So do people who are thirty pounds overweight. Successful entrepreneurs think and feel and have relationships with other people. So do those who are unemployed or even living on the streets. People who make lots of money read books. People who are broke read books, too.

Winners and losers both do the same basic things in their lives, day in and day out. Yet the things winners do take them to the top, while the things losers do take them down and out.

So what's the difference? The difference is their awareness, understanding and use of the Slight Edge in their life and work.

Successful winners understand the Slight Edge.

Unsuccessful people do not.

The difference that will make *all* the difference between success and failure, between achieving the quality of life you want and settling for less than you desire and deserve, lies one hundred percent in which of those little, "insignificant" actions you choose to do. This is why we are all capable of doing what it takes to be successful. We are all capable of being winners ... and yes, that includes you.

The Slight Edge is always working. For you or against you, the Slight Edge is already, always at work in all our lives. The purpose of this book is to help you become aware of it—how it is working in your life, every day, every hour, every moment, in every step you take and every choice you make.

Easy to Do ... Easy Not to Do

Everything you need to do to transform your life is easy to do.

It's easy to become healthy, fit and vibrant. It's easy to become financially independent. It's easy to have a happy family and a life rich with meaningful friendships.

Tapping into the Slight Edge means doing things that are easy. Simple little disciplines that, done consistently over time, will add up to the very biggest accomplishments.

It's easy to have everything you ever wanted in your life. Every action you need to take to make any and all of your dreams come true is easy. So why is it, then, that the masses are unhappy, unhealthy and financially bound?

Every action that any of these goals requires is easy to do. Here's the problem: every action that is easy to do, is also easy not to do.

Why are these simple yet crucial things easy not to do? Because if you don't do them, they won't kill you ... at least, not today. You won't suffer, or fail or blow it—today. Something is easy not to do when it won't bankrupt you, destroy your career, ruin your relationships or wreck your health—today.

What's more, not doing it is usually more comfortable than doing it would be. But that simple, seemingly insignificant error in judgment, compounded over time, *will* kill you. It will destroy you and ruin your chances for success. You can count on it. It's the Slight Edge.

That's the choice you face every day, every hour:

A simple, positive action, repeated over time.

A simple error in judgment, repeated over time.

You can always count on the Slight Edge. And unless you make it work for you, the Slight Edge *will* work against you.

Invisible Results

If I could have had a magic wand that day in the Phoenix airport as I sat thinking and having my shoes shined, one of the first things I would have done would have been to wave it at the little pile of paperbacks. I would have waved the wand and *Presto!* Now there would be a little reading table piled with Napoleon Hill, James Allen, Stephen Covey and George S. Clason. Because the simple truth is, how you feed your mind is every bit as critical to your happiness as how you feed your body.

Seeing how naturally open-minded and intellectually curious the shoeshine woman was, I have no doubt she would have dove into any one of these books with gusto.

But then we would have run into a problem.

Everything you need to know to be successful—every how-to, every practical action—is already written in books like these. Here's a Slight Edge action guaranteed to change your life: read just ten pages of a good book, a book aimed at improving your life, every day.

If you read ten pages of a good book today, will your life change? Of course not. If you don't read ten pages of a good book today, will your life fall apart? Of course not.

I could tell my shoeshine friend that if she would agree to read ten pages of one of these good books every single day, over time, she could not help but accumulate all the knowledge she'd ever need to be as successful as she ever wanted to be—successful enough to send her daughter to that cheerleading camp and hey, to send her to the best college in the country if she wanted. Like a penny over time, reading ten pages a day would compound, just like that, and create a ten-million-dollar bank of knowledge in her.

Would she do it? On day 1, sure. And day 2. And maybe day 3. But would she still be doing it by the end of the week?

If she did keep reading, over the course of the year she would have read 3,650 pages—the equivalent of one or two dozen books of life-transforming material! Would her life have changed? Absolutely. No question. But here, back in week 1, all that's still an *invisible result*.

Suppose she got so excited about what I told her that she persuaded one of the janitors to join her reading club. Now he agrees also to read ten pages a day. After a few days, she notices something. Her janitor friend, the one who's reading ten pages a day, and her other janitor friend, the one who isn't? No difference!

And that is exactly why most people never learn to recognize or understand the Slight Edge, the reason most people never learn how to make the Slight Edge work for them, and why the Slight Edge ends up working against them:

When you make the right choice, you won't see the results. At least, not today.

We live in a result-focused world. We expect to see results, and we expect to see them now. Push the button, the light flicks on. Step on the scale, look in the mirror, check the account balance online 24/7. *Give me feedback, trip a sensor, hit a buzzer, tell me, tell me, tell me it's working!*

But that's not how success is built. *Success is the progressive realization of a worthy ideal.* "Progressive" means success is a process, not a destination. It's something you experience gradually, over time. And here's how real success is built: *by the time you get the feedback, the real work's already done.* When you get to the point where everyone else can see your results, tell you what good choices you've made, notice your good fortune, slap you on the back and tell you how lucky you are, the critical Slight Edge choices you made are ancient history. And chances are, at the time you actually made those choices, nobody noticed but you. And even you wouldn't have noticed—unless you understood the Slight Edge.

Invisible results.

The Cost of Waiting

I'm sure you've heard about the power of compounding interest before. In fact, you've probably heard about it many times. What makes this time different?

Nothing—unless you act on it.

The single most important thing I can tell you about the Slight Edge is this: it's already working, *right now*, either for you or against you. So don't wait.

My hope for you—my request for you—is that before you reach the last page of this book, you will have put in place a Slight Edge financial plan for yourself so that you are consistently building your equity. Some simple, daily (or weekly, or monthly) discipline that over time, will buy your financial freedom.

Easy to do? Surprisingly so. Easy not to do? Tragically so.

To give you a sense of the cost of waiting, look at the following example.

Let's say you and your best friend are both twenty-four years old; you both read *The Slight Edge* and decide you'd like to start putting away $2,000 a year into an IRA so you'll retire at age sixty-five with over a million dollars.

Your friend starts doing it now. You wait. You don't get around to it this year, or next, or the next ... in fact, you procrastinate for the next six years.

At the beginning of year 7, you ask your friend how his IRA is doing. You are stunned when he tells you that he's finished: after investing $2,000 a year for six years at twelve percent, he's all set. By the age of sixty-five, the little financial ball he's started rolling will have snowballed into over one million dollars—even if he never puts in another penny!

That's it, you decide, it's time for action. You start putting in your $2,000 each year. How many years will it take before you've caught up to your friend? In other words, by what age will you be able to stop investing your annual $2,000, like he did?

You can't believe your eyes when you see the answer: you're going to have to keep investing that $2,000 every single year until the age of sixty-two! Your six years of procrastination has cost you thirty-three years of investing—that's twenty-seven more years and $54,000 more invested just to arrive at the same place!

"But what if I'm not twenty-four—what if I'm forty-four? Or sixty-four? Does that mean I've missed the boat—are you saying it's too late for me?"

Not at all. You're never too old, and it's never too late, to start applying Slight Edge tactics to achieve your dreams, financial and otherwise. In fact, best-selling author David Bach has written an excellent book titled *Start Late, Finish Rich*, addressing exactly that issue. Like all the other books I list in the Appendix, it's a great companion to *The Slight Edge*. My point is simply that there is a cost to waiting.

It's never too late to start.

It's always too late to wait.

The Cost of Waiting

	Your Friend			You	
Age	Payment	Accum. Total	Payment		Accum. Total
24	$2,000	$2,240	0		0
25	2,000	4,749	0		0
26	2,000	7,559	0		0
27	2,000	10,706	0		0
28	2,000	14,230	0		0
29	2,000	18,178	0		0
30	0	20,359	$2,000		$2,240
31	0	22,803	2,000		4,749
32	0	25,539	2,000		7,559
33	0	28,603	2,000		10,706
34	0	32,036	2,000		14,230
35	0	35,880	2,000		18,178
36	0	40,186	2,000		22,599
37	0	45,008	2,000		27,551
38	0	50,409	2,000		33,097
39	0	56,458	2,000		39,309
40	0	63,233	2,000		46,266
41	0	70,821	2,000		54,058
42	0	79,320	2,000		62,785
43	0	88,838	2,000		72,559
44	0	99,499	2,000		83,507
45	0	111,438	2,000		95,767
46	0	124,811	2,000		109,499
47	0	139,788	2,000		124,879
48	0	156,563	2,000		142,105
49	0	175,351	2,000		161,397
50	0	196,393	2,000		183,005
51	0	219,960	2,000		207,206
52	0	246,355	2,000		234,310
53	0	275,917	2,000		264,668
54	0	309,028	2,000		298,668
55	0	346,111	2,000		336,748
56	0	387,644	2,000		379,398
57	0	434,161	2,000		427,166
58	0	486,261	2,000		480,665
59	0	544,612	2,000		540,585
60	0	609,966	2,000		607,695
61	0	683,162	2,000		682,859
62	0	765,141	2,000		767,042
63	0	856,958	0		861,327
64	0	959,793	0		966,926
65	0	$1,074,968	0		$1,085,197

What You Do Matters

I am as passionate about personal health and fitness as I am about financial health. I believe your health is your most prized possession. It amazes me how many people pay no attention to their health.

Do you know anyone who would eat a quart of Crisco or a pound of butter a day? *Hey, my cholesterol's down to 239, I need to get it up over 400. There are still a few arteries flowing and I need to get 'em all clogged, right now, today!* Does anyone believe that's the way to good health? Of course not. Then why do we act like we do?

You know what you're supposed to eat. We all do. Fresh fruits and vegetables, complex carbs, salads, whole foods, lean meats, more fish and poultry than beef ... You know it, I know it, we all know it. So why do so many of us still go out and chow down cheeseburgers and fries every day?

I'll tell you why: because it won't kill us. Not today.

If you ate a cheeseburger and immediately suffered a near-fatal heart attack, would you ever go near a cheeseburger again? I doubt it. It may take twenty or thirty years, but when you add up the compounded interest on all that high-fat, artery-clogging dietary mayhem, eventually your poor overworked heart just quits, stops dead. And so do you. We dig our graves with our teeth.

It's easy to eat well. And it's easy not to.

It's not the one junk-food meal; it's the thousands, over time. Eating the burger is just a simple error in judgment. Not eating it, a simple positive action. Eating it won't kill you—today. But compounded over time, it can and will. Not eating it won't save you—today. But compounded over time, it can and will.

A simple, positive action. A simple error in judgment. Either way, it's the Slight Edge at work—working for you or working against you.

Invisible results.

Why do you walk past the exercise bike? Because it's easy. If you don't exercise today, will that kill you? No, of course not. You know what you need to do to stay healthy and feel fit and live a long life. Get your heart rate up, a little over normal, for twenty minutes, three times a week. You know it, I know it, everyone knows it. And it's easy to do.

But it's also easy not to do. And if you don't do it today, or tomorrow, or the next day, you won't suddenly drop dead, and you won't suddenly put on twenty pounds, and you won't suddenly lose all your muscle tone and flop around like a marionette with his strings cut off. But that simple error in judgment, compounded over time, will take you down and out.

It is the same with your health, your diet, your exercise, your financial habits, your knowledge, your relationships, your marriage. With anything and everything. With your life.

You see one person eating a good meal, and the person next to him eating an awful meal. One person saving a penny, another spending a penny. One taking a brisk walk, another sitting and watching the news. Is there any difference between the two? Nothing you can see ... not today, and probably not tomorrow. It's easy to conclude that it doesn't really make any difference.

The difference between success and failure is not dramatic. In fact, the difference between success and failure is so subtle, most people miss it. They hold the philosophy that what they do doesn't really matter. It's not hard to see how people come to this understanding of life. I don't blame them. It's completely understandable. It's just not the truth.

The truth is, what you do matters. What you do today matters. What you do every day matters.

Those little things that will make you successful in life, that will secure your health, your happiness, your fulfillment, your dreams, are simple, subtle, tiny things that nobody will see, nobody will applaud, nobody will even notice. They are those things that, at the time you do them, often feel like they make absolutely no difference ... like they don't matter.

They do.

CHAPTER 3

The Secret of Time

There is a tide in the affairs of men
Which, taken at the flood, leads on to fortune;
Omitted, all the voyage of their life
Is bound in shallows and in miseries.
— William Shakespeare, *Julius Caesar*

So you walk a little today, get your heart rate up a bit, you lift a few weights, you eat a little differently, then tomorrow morning you wake up and look in the mirror ... and see the same old flubber. You have to be pretty well along the path to see any significant results. What keeps you doing this simple thing, day after day?

Will power! It's like my dad (mom, teacher, boss, older brother, minister, self) always told me ... I just need more will power.

Really? I don't think so. (A friend of mine used to say that people on diets who complain that they lack will power are usually suffering more from a lack of *won't* power!) Will power is vastly overrated. For most people, will power ends up looking and feeling like some sort of grim self-tyranny, and involves creating an elaborate, artificial reward-and-punishment system.

Do you want to change? If so, I can show you how to tap into the most powerful force for change there is. Would you like to know what it is? Are you ready? Here it is:

TIME.

Position your daily actions so time is working for instead of against you. Because time will either promote you or expose you.

What keeps you on the path is your Slight Edge philosophy, which includes your understanding of the secret of time. Knowing the secret of time, you say, *If I stay on this road long enough, I'll get the result I seek.* It's not a question of your mood, your feelings or your attitude. And it's not a question of will power. It's a question of simply *knowing*.

When you enter a darkened room, why does your hand reach out for the light switch? Because you know that when you hit the switch, the light will go on. You don't have to give yourself positive self-talk about how you really ought to hit that light switch, or set up a system of rewards and punishments for yourself around whether you follow through or not with hitting the light switch. You don't need any rigmarole; you just hit the switch. Why? Because you know what will happen.

You *know*.

It's the exact same thing here: you walk a little every day, lift a few weights, eat a little better, and leave the penny in the purse (hit the light switch) because you know it will make you healthy and wealthy (the light will turn on).

It's the exact same thing, no different—except for one thing, and that is time.

"Instant Life"

If you were offered the same choice the wealthy man gave his sons, would you choose the million dollars or the penny? Most people would make the second boy's choice: the right-now money. After all, a million dollars! In cash! Right now!

And, of course, you'd be making the wrong choice—and you would have been fooled, as millions of people around the globe are fooled every minute of every hour of every day, by those two seductive little words:

Right now!

I remember one day, years ago when microwave ovens were still somewhat of a novelty, seeing a man standing in front of a microwave, fidgeting impatiently as he peered through the window at his lunch being cooked, and muttering, "Come onnnn ... come onnnn ... !"

It blew my mind. Sixty seconds wasn't fast enough?!

It's become a truism to say we live in a push-button, instant-gratification world, but this is a truth very much worth pondering, because it doesn't simply mean we have more impatient temperaments than our parents do. It represents an entirely different way of thinking. An entirely different philosophy.

There is a natural progression in life, which everyone knew intimately back in the days when we were an agrarian society. You plant, then you cultivate, and finally you harvest. Plant, cultivate, harvest.

In today's word, everyone wants to go directly from plant to harvest. We plant the seed by joining the gym, and then get frustrated when a few days go by and there's no fitness harvest. Taking recreational drugs is an effort to go from plant directly to harvest. So is taking steroids to enhance athletic performance. So is robbing a bank; so is playing the lottery.

The step we keep overlooking (and overskipping!) is the step of cultivating. And that, unlike planting and harvesting, takes place only through the patient dimension of time.

Because we are a culture raised on television and movies, we've lost track of time. We don't understand time any more. I'm not criticizing television and films. Film is an amazing art form, television is a powerful medium, and in the hands of true artists, they can both teach us valuable lessons about life. Just not about time.

Through a great film, you can experience the triumph of the human soul over adversity, the drama of a struggle between doing what's right and succumbing to the temptations of the world, a moving encounter between generations, the flowering of a powerful romance, the struggle and birth of a nation ...

But it all has to be finished in *two hours*.

Can you imagine a nation being born in two hours? Meeting the person who will become the love of your life—the dating, courtship, romance, struggle, triumph, wedding and life thereafter—in two hours? Of course not. But in a world filled with instant coffee, instant breakfast, instant credit, instant shopping, instant news and instant information, we have come dangerously close to losing touch with reality and believing we have access to *instant life*.

Past generations learned about life through books. Books take time to read. When John Irving adapted his novel, *The Cider House*

Rules, to the screen, he collapsed the time frame. The story in the
novel takes fifteen years; the story in the film takes fifteen months.
James Grady's novel *Six Days of the Condor* was turned into a film:
Three Days of the Condor. A child who a generation ago might have
spent a month reading Charles Dickens's great coming-of-age
novel *Great Expectations* can now catch the 1998 version on cable
and gobble it up in one hour and fifty-one minutes.

In a film, we never see the little steps, repeated hundreds of
times, which create the result. There isn't time. We might see a
quick sequence of steps that conveys a super-compressed sense of
the evolution of the thing—the "falling in love montage" in practically every romantic comedy, or the "training sequence" in every
sports movie. But these little Slight Edge–like dramas never last
longer than thirty or forty seconds!

In real life, everything important happens through time.
Success, remember, is the progressive realization of a worthy
ideal. All generations born since the advent of television (and
especially since the rapid-cutting style of MTV stepped up the
pace) have a hard time grasping that. Which is one reason the
Slight Edge is more important than ever.

Where's the Drama?

It's not that becoming aware of the Slight Edge will make these
critical choices easier—because they're already easy! And that,
oddly enough, is the challenge of it. This is not about making
tough choices. It's about making easy choices.

The problem is, making the wrong choices—the ones that
will tilt the Slight Edge to lean against you instead of in your
favor—are also easy choices.

In a way, it would be a simpler matter if making the right
choices were a big deal. If it were a dramatic, huge, difficult thing.
Why? Because then it would be obvious. You wouldn't need this
book. The challenge is that making the right choices is not dramatic. When the hero makes the right choice in a movie, it's dramatic, all right. Problem is, your life is not a movie. It's real life.

Deciding whether or not to kill Darth Vader with your light
saber is a dramatic choice. Deciding whether or not to fasten your
seat belt is an undramatic, boring, mundane little choice that
nobody will even witness. But guess which choice has the power

to take a few hundred thousand lives each year? Hint: it's not the light saber.

If making the right Slight Edge choices were a dramatic thing, you'd get *immediate feedback*. An entire movie theater audience applauding, cheering or screaming. But that doesn't happen. And that's the big challenge of it: no immediate feedback.

The right choices and wrong choices you make at the moment will have little or no noticeable impact on how your day goes for you. Nor tomorrow, nor the next day. No applause, no cheers, no screams, no life-or-death results played out in Technicolor. But it is precisely those very same, undramatic, seemingly insignificant actions that, when compounded over time, will *dramatically* affect how your life turns out.

So, where's the drama? It comes at the end of the story, when the credits start to roll—which comes not in two hours but in two years. Or, depending on what Slight Edge and what particular story we're talking about, perhaps twelve years, or twenty-two.

Making the right choices, taking the right actions. It's truly easy to do. Ridiculously easy. But it's just as easy not to do. And if you don't do them, there won't be any big drama about it. It won't kill you; it won't hurt you; in fact, it won't make any difference at all ...

Not today, anyway. Not tomorrow. But over time?

The right choices you make today, compounded over time, will take you higher and higher up the success curve of this real-time movie called "your life." The wrong choices you make today, compounded over time, will absolutely, positively and inevitably

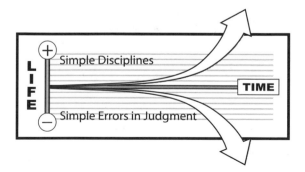

take you down and out.

Either way, there *will* be dramatic results, just like in a movie. Unlike a movie, it will just take time before you see them.

Making the Choice to Make the Choice

For twenty-one years, the wealthy man gave his sons everything he had, including all his love, all his care and a magnificent place to live. But when they turned twenty-one, he gave them the most valuable gift of all. He gave them a choice.

That most valuable gift of all is a gift that you always have. You always have a choice.

No matter what you have done in your life up until today, no matter where you are and how far down you may have slid on the failure curve, you can start fresh, building a positive pattern of success, at any time. Including right now.

But you need to have faith in the process, because *you won't see it happening at first.*

If you base your choices on the evidence, on what you can see, you're sunk. You need to base your choices on your philosophy—on what you know, not what you see.

The Slight Edge is like Lady Justice, the famous blindfolded statue. The statue itself, of the woman holding the scales and sword, has been around since the days of ancient Rome. The blindfold was added in the sixteenth century, in the years leading up to that era we call the "Enlightenment" that gave birth to modern ideas of representative democracy and universal human rights. The blindfold is not meant to signify that justice is "blind," as people sometimes assume, but that true justice is impervious to external influence.

That also makes it a very good representation of the Slight Edge.

If you want to understand and apply the Slight Edge to create the life of your dreams, you can't make your choices based on the evidence of your eyes. You need to make them based on what you know. On your philosophy.

Picture success and failure as the two sides of a pair of balance scales, like the one held by Lady Justice.

Let's say you're in a tough place in your life. The scales are tipped badly, the negative side tilted way down. Whether it's your health, or your finances, or your marriage, or your career ... whatever it is, you've reached a place where many years of simple errors in judgment have compounded over time, and you're feeling it. You're behind the eight ball. It sure would be nice if, somehow, you could do something dramatic. If you just wake up tomorrow and have it all turned around—snap your fingers and change it.

That might happen, in a movie. But this is your life. What can you do?

What happens if you add one small, simple, positive action to the success side? Nothing you can see. What happens if you add one more? Nothing you can see. What happens if you keep adding one more, and one more, and one more, and one more ...

Before too long, you see the scales shift, ever so slightly. And then again. And eventually, that heavy "failure" side starts to lift, and lift, and lift ... and the scales start swinging your way. No matter how much negative weight from the past is on the other side, just by adding those little grams of success, one at a time (and by *not* adding more weight to the failure side), you will eventually and inevitably begin to shift the scales in your favor.

Way back in the beginning, when you add the first few morsels of positive action, if you judge your choices by the evidence of your eyes, you won't see the scales move at all and that will frustrate you. It frustrates nineteen out of twenty people so much, they quit. And that is the saddest thing I can think of.

The Power of Compounding Effort

Picture a huge, heavy flywheel—a massive metal disk mounted horizontally on an axle, about thirty feet in diameter, two feet thick, and weighing about 5,000 pounds. Now imagine that your task is to get the flywheel rotating on the axle as fast and for as long as possible.

Pushing with great effort, you get the flywheel to inch forward, moving almost imperceptibly at first. You keep pushing and, after two or three hours of persistent effort, you get the flywheel to complete one entire turn.

You keep pushing, and the flywheel begins to move a bit faster, and with continued great effort, you move it round a second rotation. You keep pushing in a consistent direction. Three turns ... four ... five ... six ... the flywheel builds up speed ... seven

... eight ... you keep pushing ... nine ... ten ... it builds momentum ... eleven ... twelve ... moving faster with each turn ... twenty ... thirty ... fifty... a hundred.

Then at some point—breakthrough! The momentum of the thing kicks in your favor, hurling the flywheel forward, turn after turn ... whoosh! ... its own heavy weight working for you. You're pushing no harder than the first rotation, but the flywheel goes faster and faster. Each turn of the flywheel builds upon work done earlier, compounding your investment of effort. A thousand times faster, then ten thousand, then a hundred thousand. The huge heavy disk flies forward with almost unstoppable momentum.

Now suppose someone came along and asked, "What was the one big push that caused this thing to go so fast?"

You wouldn't be able to answer; it's a nonsensical question. Was it the first push? The second? The fifth? The hundredth? No! It was *all* of them added together in an overall accumulation of effort applied in a consistent direction. Some pushes may have been bigger than others, but any single heave—no matter how large—reflects a small fraction of the entire cumulative effect upon the flywheel.

— From *Good to Great: Why Some Companies Make the Leap ... and Others Don't*, by Jim Collins, HarperBusiness, NY (2001); pp 165–6.

Successful people do whatever it takes to get the job done, whether or not they feel like it. They understand that it is not any one single push on the flywheel, but the cumulative total of all their sequential, unfailingly consistent pushes that eventually creates movement of such astonishing momentum in their lives.

Successful people form habits that feed their success, instead of habits that feed their failure. They choose to have the Slight Edge working for them, not against them. They build their own dreams, rather than spend their lives building other people's dreams, and they achieve these dramatic results in their lives through making choices that are the very antithesis of drama—mundane, simple, seemingly insignificant choices.

Every decision you make is a Slight Edge decision. What you're going to do, how you're going to act, what you're going to read, who you're going to chat with on the phone, what you're going to eat for lunch, who you're going to associate with. How you're going to treat your fellow workers. What you're going to get done today.

Simply by making those right decisions, or making more of them—one at a time, over and over again—you will have enlisted the awesome power of the Slight Edge on your behalf. The unwanted circumstances, the poor results you've produced in the past, and the evidence of failures in your life, may all continue for a time. There may be no light at the end of the tunnel, or at least none you can see today. But by putting time on your side, you've marshaled the forces of the Slight Edge. Your success becomes inevitable. You just need to stay in the process long enough to give it a chance to win.

It starts with a choice.

Patience and Faith

Patience is a challenge for people who do not understand the Slight Edge.

Often, in the beginning, the success path can be uncomfortable, even scary. Especially if you're the only one around who's on it. And with only one out of twenty people ever achieving their goals, it's quite likely that you *will* be the only one around on the path—at least for a while.

Sometimes the path of success is inconvenient, and therefore easier not to do. For most people, it's easier to stay in bed. Getting on the path and staying on the path requires faith in the process— especially at the start. That makes you a pioneer.

Pioneers don't know what's out there, but out there, they go anyway. That's why being a pioneer takes such courage. *Courage* means to have a purpose and to have heart. Once you are aware of and understand how to use the Slight Edge, you will naturally have both—purpose and the strength of heart to stay on that purpose.

The important point is to start on the path and to remember that no matter what has gone on before, you can begin fresh and new any time you choose. You can start with a clean slate.

How long will it take? How long before you will actually see and feel (and smell and touch and be able to spend and enjoy and appreciate) the results? How long before you will have the experience of the success you're seeking?

Obviously, it's impossible for either of us to say exactly how long. But the truth is, in three to five years, you can put virtually anything in your life onto the right track. Think of what you were doing three years ago: it seems like yesterday, doesn't it? Well, three years from now, the things you're doing right now will seem like only yesterday, too. Yet this brief little period of time can change your life.

How long will it take? Chances are it will take longer than you want it to ... and when the time arrives, you'll be astonished at how quick it seemed.

Patience is not an issue for the water hyacinth. It simply goes about its business, calmly, quietly doubling, until it covers the pond. You can do the same.

> Serene, I fold my hands and wait,
> Nor care for wind, nor tide, nor sea;
> I rave no more 'gainst time or fate,
> For lo! my own shall come to me.
>
> —John Burroughs, *Waiting*

The Slight Edge guarantees that *your own shall come to you*, like the water hyacinth covering the pond. The way your own shows up, good or bad, failure or success, win or lose, is, moment by moment, up to you. You need not "care for wind, or tide, or sea ..." —but you do need to care for those simple little actions which, compounded over time, will make the difference between your success or failure.

The problem is that most of us live with one foot planted firmly in the past and the other tucked timidly in the future— never in the moment. In relation to everything—our kids, our health, our home, our career—we tick through the hours in constant regret and Monday-morning-quarterbacking about what's behind us, and with worry, anxiety and dread about what lies ahead.

The Slight Edge is all about living in the moment. It is perhaps the hardest lesson to learn about the Slight Edge: you can't find it in the past or the future, only right here, right now.

The reason Ekhart Tolle's modest little 1997 book on enlightenment, *The Power of Now*, took the marketplace by storm, selling over two million copies in thirty languages, is that his core message is one that everyone knows they need to hear: *your life exists only in the moment.* But you can't really absorb or live that truth through reading a book; you absorb and live that truth simply by being fully in the process of living your life—not regretting the past, not dreading the future.

The Slight Edge is about your awareness. It is about you making the right choices, the choices that serve you and empower you, starting right now and continuing for the rest of your life, and learning to make them effortlessly.

This book is about putting the Slight Edge to work for you, instead of against you.

It's easy to do. And it's easy not to do. And if you don't do it, it won't kill you or destroy your chances for success today. But that simple error in judgment, compounded over time, will kill your chances for success. It will take you down and out of your life forever. And that choice is always yours.

The choice of simple things, and the wisdom to make that choice. The wealthy man was right: the third gift is one that you can only claim; it's something nobody can *give* you.

It's also something no one can take *away* from you.

CHAPTER 4

The Secret of the Penny

To see a world in a grain of sand,
And a heaven in a wild flower,
Hold infinity in the palm of your hand,
And eternity in an hour ...
— William Blake, *Auguries of Innocence*

I've presented the story of the penny doubled every day to hundreds and hundreds of audiences, and often I hear a comment like this:

Wow, that's amazing ... to think that you could start with nothing and build a fortune!

That's not quite accurate: you don't start with nothing. You start with a penny.

No big deal, I mean, of course, you start with a penny, but, you know, it's basically starting with nothing.

No, it's not: it's starting with a penny. It may seem like an insignificant difference (although you're probably starting to have a little bit different view of the word "insignificant"). The truth is, it makes *all* the difference.

You Have to Start with a Penny

To accomplish anything worth accomplishing, to create success, to achieve your dreams, you don't have to do impossible, extraordinary, superhuman things. But you have to do *something*. You have to start with a penny.

Success doesn't come from nowhere; it can't be conjured up out of thin air. It comes from a very small, tiny beginning—but there has to be a beginning. That beginning is the thing people miss, the thing they don't see. And they don't see it because it's so tiny, it's almost invisible.

A dead-broke, struggling young English teacher named Steve had started writing a story about a troubled high-school girl. Within a handful of pages, he realized the story wasn't working out and tossed the pages in the trash. Why add yet one more to his large and growing stack of rejection notices?

The next day, as Steve's wife was doing some straightening up, she bent down to empty his trash basket and happened to notice the curled little sheaf of papers. She straightened them out, dusted off the cigarette ashes, read them and took them to Steve: she thought he maybe had something worth finishing.

She was right. He did finish it, and the paperback rights sold for nearly a half a million dollars. What's more, his story of the troubled school girl named Carrie launched Stephen King's career: he became the most successful writer in the twentieth century.

What Tabitha King recognized in the trash may have been a tarnished penny, but still, it was a penny.

One chilly day in December 1955, an unknown forty-two-year-old seamstress in Montgomery, Alabama decided she'd had enough. She was tired after a long day's work. Most of all, she was tired of being treated the way she was—and tired of every other person of her color being treated that way, too. So when she was told to give up her bus seat to a white passenger, she refused—even when the bus driver threatened her with arrest.

It was no idle threat; she was arrested, then convicted and fined for violating a city ordinance. Her case was the catalyst for the formation of a new civil rights organization. On the same day of the woman's hearing, the newly formed Montgomery Improvement Association elected a young and relatively unknown minister named Martin Luther King, Jr., to be its spokesperson, launching a movement that over the next decade abolished legal segregation and radically transformed the face of the nation.

Rosa Parks was a penny.

Let's do one more bit of time travel. There was a time, a certain number of years ago, when a tiny blob of gelatin began to pulse with hidden potential. It was barely more than a speck of matter, about the thickness of a dollar bill, at the very threshold of human sight: any smaller and it would have been invisible to the naked eye.

Though tiny, this insignificant little dot of matter (you could have fit about twenty of them on the head of a pin) contained chemical instructions that, if printed out, would have filled more than 500,000 pages; in fact, it was among the most organized, complex structures in the universe. Over the next nine months of Slight Edge compounding, this little blob of gelatin would blossom into over thirty trillion cells before being born into the open air ... and letting out a wail as it took its first breath.

It would become you.

You started as a penny.

"God Is in the Details"

There is an old expression, "the Devil is in the details," which people usually take to mean something like, "Make sure you read the print before you sign the contract!" The legendary architect Mies van der Rohe had a different take on it; he said, "God is in the details." They're both absolutely right. God or Devil, for good or for ill, better or worse, sickness or health, success or failure ... the critical decisions in life are always the tiny ones. Which is exactly why most people miss them.

Since I've mentioned God, there's a great passage in the Old Testament that speaks volumes about the truth of the Slight Edge. It's in the story of the prophet Elijah, who is one of the most dramatic characters in the entire Old Testament (which is something that I think makes the story especially significant).

Elijah has run for his life into the wilderness and holed up in a cave, when a voice comes to him and tells him to go outside and meet the Lord. He's about to step out of the cave, when he stops and thinks, he really ought to follow those directions pretty carefully. So he decides to wait until he knows the Lord is actually out there before he goes out to greet him.

After a few minutes, he hears a rushing sound, then a rising wail that crescendos to an unearthly scream—and a few seconds later a hurricane-force wind comes wailing through! But he doesn't budge. Why? Because impressive though the hurricane is, Elijah knows it's just a hurricane. "The Lord was not in the wind."

After the hurricane recedes, the place starts shaking and trembling. Pieces of rock start breaking off the cave walls and ceiling and falling at his feet, and next thing you know Elijah is witnessing an earthquake! But he holds his ground, because "the Lord was not in the earthquake."

Finally, after the last tremors of the earthquake die down, Elijah hears an eerie hissing sound. He feels the air around him growing hotter and hotter, and suddenly the mouth of the cave is illuminated by an intense reddish-orange glow—the whole place outside is in flames, as if a gigantic conflagration, like the mother of all forest fires, is moving past! But Elijah still refuses to budge. And sure enough, he's right again: "the Lord was not in the fire."

And what comes after the hurricane, and the earthquake, and the massive fire? Nothing. Nothing at all; only silence. Well, almost nothing. Maybe there's just this tiny sound—"a still, small voice." Almost too quiet to hear, so quiet that Elijah can't quite make out what it's saying, only that it's there ...

And without hesitating, he steps out of the cave. (*I Kings 19:12*)

After all that din, clamor and drama, that "still, small" sound would have been very easy to miss—or to dismiss. "Did I hear something ... nahh, it's probably nothing." And in that tiny sound was all of Creation speaking!

By the way, the Old Testament isn't the only place where you'll find vividly told Slight Edge stories. All traditional wisdom books, from Scriptures and holy books, to ancient heroic epics, to fables and fairy tales, are brimming with Slight Edge wisdom. Once you understand the Slight Edge, you start to see the collected experience and observations of sacred and folk traditions in a whole new light.

A Penny for Your Thoughts ...

Now imagine that instead of a penny doubling every day, it's your health that you're increasing by one penny's worth ... and then by two pennies, and then four.

If you could come up with something that would make you feel one penny's worth better, could you do that every day? Of course. A little moderate exercise, a brisk one-mile walk, a quarter of an hour on a treadmill, not going that fast. Get your heart rate up slightly, no big deal.

And your reward? When you get up the next morning, do you feel better? Not really. I mean, not noticeably. Maybe just a little ... say, a penny's worth. Hardly seems worth the effort. And after a week, you're feeling sixty-four cents' worth better. Big deal! You've had to put up with some rainy weather, walk through a few stiff muscles, and miss your favorite news program ... hey, it's really not worth it.

But what if you kept doing it anyway? Would you eventually feel like a million bucks? No—you'd feel like *ten* million.

But you need to start with the penny.

Now imagine that penny is your knowledge.

If I told you that reading Napoleon Hill's *Think and Grow Rich* would change your life, would you sit down and read it, cover to cover, today? Mind you, that's a 256-page book, and those aren't lightweight pages. Or another classic, Stephen Covey's *The 7 Habits of Highly Effective People.* That's a 358-pager, and it's not easy reading.

Would you read either one in a single day? I doubt it. I wouldn't—I can't spend the entire day reading, and I'll bet you can't either.

But could you read a penny's worth—say, ten pages? (Actually, at current used-book prices on amazon.com, ten pages of the Hill book would cost about fifty cents, and ten pages of the Covey would run about ten cents—but I'm using the penny here as a metaphor!) I don't know how much you would get out of ten pages; maybe a lot, maybe nothing. Let's say you get nothing. But if you could read ten pages today, could you read ten more tomorrow? Of course you could—anyone who can read could do that.

And if you do that, and you keep it up every day for a year, you will have read about a dozen brilliant, life-transforming classics. Your mind will be filled with the strategies and know-how to create a startling new level of success. You will have thoughts of millionaires—all from a penny.

But you need to start with the penny.

Let's Get Real

"Okay, doubling a penny in a story is all very well. But I don't see anyone offering to double my money every day for a month, not in real life. Besides, even if I could get compound interest on a money account, how am I supposed to add up compound interest in health, or relationships, or knowledge?"

Fair enough. Let's change the question. Forget about doubling for a minute, and let's forget about compound interest, too, for the moment. Let's just *add a penny* every day, not double the penny. Do you think you could improve yourself—your health, your knowledge, your skills, your diet, your relationships, whatever area of life you want to look at—just one percent?

Wait—before you answer that, let's make it even smaller. What if you were able to improve yourself, today, just *three-tenths* of one percent? That's a 0.003 improvement—a very Slight Edge indeed. So slight, in fact, you might have a hard time even knowing how to measure it.

Now, what if you did that again tomorrow, and the next day, and kept it up every day for the next year? Remember, you're not going to add up compound interest this time, you're just adding on another three-tenths of one percent each day.

Here's what will happen. The first day you'll improve by 0.003, so little it will probably be impossible to notice. The second day, your improvement will be 0.006; the next day, 0.009, almost a full one percent. And by the end of the year, you will have improved by one hundred percent.

Doubled.

You will be *twice* what you are today—twice as fit, twice as wealthy, twice as skilled, twice as happy ... twice as whatever it is you've been working on, in whatever areas you apply your daily three-tenths-percent effort. Twice the *you*, in just one year!

If you give yourself a year to do it, you can become twice the person you are today. Imagine having twice the net worth, twice the personal relationships, twice the health. Making twice the positive impact on the world. Having twice as much fun and enjoying twice the quality of life.

How could you possibly accomplish this? By trying twice as hard? Working twice as many hours? Have twice as positive an attitude? No—by improving three-tenths of one percent at a time.

Every day, in every moment, you get to exercise choices that will determine whether or not you will become a great person, living a great life. Greatness is not something predetermined, predestined or carved into your fate by forces beyond your control. *Greatness is always in the moment of the decision.*

But you have to start with a penny. And that's the great and tragic irony of it, the sad and terrible tale of the ninety-five percent: that little penny seems so insignificant, so small, so silly ... why even bother to bend over and pick it up? After all ...

Can you imagine walking into your bank to deposit a single penny into a savings account? Can you imagine looking in your savings account, deposit box or piggy bank, and finding a balance of $0.01? It might as well be a balance of zero, right? How much different is there, right? I mean, we're talking about one penny! What could you buy with a penny?

You just might be able to buy financial freedom for the rest of your life.

CHAPTER 5

The Quantum Leap Myth

Some day we'll say and do
Things we've been longing to;
Though she's far away
I'll find my love some day,
Some day when my dreams come true.
—from "Some Day My Prince Will Come,"
(Snow White and the Seven Dwarfs)
music by Frank Church, lyrics by Larry Morey

Some Day ...

Some day, when my ship comes in ...
Some day, when I have the money ...
Some day, when I have the time ...
Some day, when I have the skill, the confidence ...

Have I got some shocking news for you: "some day" doesn't exist, never has, and never will. There is no "some day." There's only today. When tomorrow comes, it will be another today; so will the next day. They all will. There is never anything but today.

And some more shocking news: your ship's not coming—it's already here. Docked and waiting. You already have the money. You already have the time. You already have the skill, the confidence. You already have everything you need to achieve everything you want.

You just can't see it.

Why not? Because you're looking in the wrong place. You're looking for the breakthrough, the quantum leap. You're looking for the winning lottery ticket in a game that isn't a lottery!

Have you ever noticed that when you read stories about lottery winners, they are hardly ever bank presidents, successful entrepreneurs or corporate executives? That they never seem to be people who were *already* financially successful before they bought that winning ticket? Have you ever wondered why? It's because successful people never win the lottery. Why not? Because they don't buy lottery tickets.

Successful people have already grasped the truth that lottery players have not: life is not a lottery. Success is not a random accident.

Greek Gods and Real Heroes

In ancient Greek theater, characters generally got themselves into as much of a mess as the playwright could possibly dream up. Everything would be headed for an absolutely impossible disaster when (in the last few minutes of the play) an actor playing a "god" would come floating down from the sky to make everything right—banishing this character and reinstating that one, punishing another and granting divine clemency to still another, explaining the inexplicable and solving the insoluble.

Things would be in such a mess, there'd be no way a human being could sort the stuff out. Obviously, it would have to take a being with divine powers. And just like in a stage production of *Peter Pan*, the actor would be suspended by ropes and a system of pulleys, a mechanical contrivance they termed a "machine," or *machina*.

Today, thousands of years later, people still refer to a last-minute "cheat" solution for an impossible problem coming out of thin air as a deus ex machina, or "god dropping in out of nowhere by a machine"—the supernatural, breakthrough force that pops in just to make all things right. And by the way, when critics say a play, novel or film uses a "deus ex machina," it's not a compliment! It's their way of saying, "Oh yeah, right. Couldn't come up with real solution, huh, so you had to trot in a *deus ex machina?* Gimme a break!"

And that is just what it is people are hoping for: a break. The big break. The lucky break. The breakthrough. A break in the routine ... a break with reality. A deus ex machina. But that's not how things really work.

Okay, then, how do things really work?

Look at some of the real-world problems that would have made Athena or Apollo or any other deity of Greek drama pull their hair out.

William Wilberforce spent his entire career introducing bill after bill to his colleagues in the British Parliament in his efforts to end slavery, only to have them defeated one after the other. From 1788 to 1806, he introduced a new anti-slavery motion and watched it fail every single year for eighteen years in a row. Finally, three days before Wilberforce's death in 1833, Parliament passed a bill to abolish slavery not only in England but also throughout its colonies. Three decades later, a similar bill would pass in the United States (spearheaded by another man of conscience who had also spent much of his life failing): Abraham Lincoln's Emancipation Proclamation.

Deus ex machina? Far from it. These were human problems, and they had human solutions. But the only access to them is through the Slight Edge.

Of course Wilberforce and Lincoln were not the sole figures in this heroic struggle, and even after their bills were passed into law on both sides of the Atlantic, the evils of slavery and racism were far from over. But their efforts—like Mother Teresa's efforts to end poverty, Gandhi's to end colonial oppression, or Martin Luther King's and Nelson Mandela's to end racism—are classic examples of what "breakthrough" looks like in the real world.

All of these real-life heroes understood the Slight Edge. None of them was hypnotized by the allure of the "big break." If they had been, they would never had continued taking the actions they took—and what would the world look like today?

One Small Step ...

Our cultural mythology, the philosophy our society subscribes to as a group, worships the breakthrough even when we don't realize that's what we're doing.

"One small step for a man ... "—nonsense! That wasn't one small step—the guy was on the moon! That was one gigantic step for man, a genuine breakthrough.

The small step was when some guy—someone you and I never heard of—first started tinkering with design ideas for how a rocket ship might withstand the intense conditions of space flight. There were thousands, hundreds of thousands, millions of "one small steps" for years and years beforehand that all went into that epic 1969 leap of Neil Armstrong's that was televised throughout the world (and is still played over and over in our culture as one of the most deeply ingrained news bites of history).

But we don't celebrate any of those real "small steps." We don't even know what they are, or who made them.

The myth of our culture is the giant step, the larger-than-life leap, the heroic effort. "Faster than a speeding bullet, able to ... " Wait, how does that go again? Is it, "able to take small, insignificant, incremental steps, consistently, over time?" No, it's "able to leap tall buildings in a single bound!" I mean, what kind of Superman would take tiny steps?

The kind who wins. Like Edison and his light bulb.

There's a popular expression these days, "Luck is preparedness meeting opportunity." It's a nifty little saying, and it's close, but in my experience, it isn't quite accurate. Luck is preparedness—period! Preparedness through doing those simple, little, constructive, positive actions, over and over. Luck is preparedness that eventually creates opportunity!

That's the truth of big breaks, lucky breaks and breakthroughs: they do happen—just not out of thin air.

Have you ever suddenly understood something in a "flash of recognition"? Have you ever known of someone who became an "overnight success"? Here is a secret: both that "sudden flash" and that "overnight success" were the final, breakthrough results of a lengthy process of edge upon edge upon edge. You may completely and absolutely trust in the truth that it is always the little things, done consistently over time, which bring about the "breakthroughs" that you see.

No success is immediate. Nor is any failure instantaneous. They are both products of the Slight Edge.

The truth of quantum leaps is that they are not larger than life: they're submicroscopic. The actual term "quantum leap" comes from particle physics, where it does not refer to a huge, epic jump. It refers to the fact that energy, after a period of time, will suddenly appear at another level, without our having been able to observe how it got there.

It is an exact description of how the water hyacinth moves from day twenty-nine to day thirty. An exact description of how the frog's certain death by drowning was suddenly transformed into salvation by butter.

A real-life quantum leap is not Superman leaping a tall building. A real quantum leap is Edison perfecting the electric light bulb—and transforming the world with it.

The "Magic Bullet"

Every single January in every gym in America, hundreds of thousands of people start over in a process that they will soon quit—only because they haven't set themselves up with the right expectation. They aren't looking for incremental progress; they're looking for results they can feel. They're looking for a breakthrough. They never had a chance.

Easy to do, easy not to do ... and in that tiny, seemingly insignificant little choice *not to do*, so many people needlessly live out lives of quiet desperation.

Believing in the "big break" is worse than simply being futile. It's actually dangerous, because it can keep you from taking the actions you need to take to create the results you want. It can even be lethal. Think of the poor frog that gave up and let himself drown because he couldn't see a breakthrough on the horizon. He was wrong, of course: there are miracles, even in the life of a frog. It's just that the breakthrough didn't come down out of the clouds; it came at the end of a series of consistent, determined, compounding-interest foot-paddlings.

What's the greatest gift you can give to an inner-city kid? An understanding of the Slight Edge. Because that's not the answer he's getting from the world around him. He believes that the only way out of his world of poverty, violence, oppression and fear is to become a sports superstar—because that's what we tell him. That's the quantum leap answer. The truth, of course, is that very, very few individuals will have the talent to break out of that world by becoming sports superstars. And deep down, every one of these kids knows that, or soon finds out ... so they give up. Why bother?

And they become victims of the Quantum Leap Myth.

Over the last several decades, it's been amazing to me how many people I've been close to have persisted in making fun of my dietary choices, exercise habits and personal development goals. The "insignificant" little things I've been doing every day for years have always struck them as funny, because they couldn't see the point. They couldn't see the results coming further on down the path.

Today I see these friends and ache for them: many now have failing health, are languishing in poor financial conditions and seem to have lost their hopes for the future. What they have a hard time seeing is that my good health isn't an accident, and their poor health isn't a stroke of bad luck. We've all gotten to where we are today the exact same way: the Slight Edge. They are victims of the Quantum Leap Myth.

Our society is sliding rapidly into an ever-increasing economic crisis of poor health. Endemic adult onset diabetes, heart disease, obesity and a score of other chronic illnesses have steadily fed a monstrously overgrown health care system, tax system and social security system—and there isn't a single "cause" anywhere in sight. As I'm writing this (early 2005), several of our most widely used over-the-counter drugs have suddenly been found to make things worse. And as cancer continues its climb, the drumbeat litany goes on as it has for decades: *A cure is just around the corner ... we're so close ... the latest research says ... with your dollars, we'll soon see a breakthrough ...*

A cure is not just around the corner. The cure is right here, under our noses and on our plates.

There is no mystery for those who know how to recognize the Slight Edge at work. Our entire health crisis is nothing but one set of little decisions, made daily and compounded daily, winning out over another set of little decisions, made daily and compounded daily.

We look for the cure, the breakthrough, the magic pill—the medical-scientific quantum leap miracle our press has dubbed the "magic bullet." But the solution already exists. It always did. Is it magic? Yes—the same magic that caused the problem: the power of daily actions, compounded over time. The magic of the Slight Edge.

There's a great line in the movie *Bruce Almighty*, when God (played by Morgan Freeman) is leaving the all-too-human Jim Carrey character to solve things on his own (and refusing to be a *deus ex machina*). He says, "You want a miracle? Be the miracle." Once you absorb the Slight Edge way of being, you'll stop looking for that quantum leap—and start building it.

The Winning Edge

The Slight Edge is the process every winner has used to succeed since the dawn of time. Winning is *always* a matter of the Slight Edge.

One of the most highly anticipated events at the Summer Olympics is the men's 100 meters. The winner of this quadrennial event can lay claim to being the fastest man in the world. At the 2004 Games in Athens, American Justin Gatlin ran a blistering 9.85 in the final heat to win the gold. The silver medalist, Portugal's Francis Obikwelu, ran 9.86. Yes, that's *one one-hundredth of a second slower—a very* Slight Edge.

Do you know what makes the difference between a .300-hitting baseball star with a multimillion-dollar contract and a .260-plus player making only an average salary? Less than one additional hit per week over the course of the season. And you know what makes the difference between getting that hit and striking out? About one quarter-inch up or down the bat.

No golf fan who watched the 2004 Master's tournament will ever forget how it ended: Phil Mickelson, winner of more tournaments over the past ten years than anyone else, with the exception of Tiger Woods, was left with a twenty-foot putt on the eighteenth hole of the final round. Miss it, even by one inch, and he would head into a playoff with the number two player in the world, Ernie Els. Make it, and he would finally silence the critics and win his first major. The putt rolled in and Mickelson had his green jacket.

Over the course of the tournament's four days, Mickelson shot a 279, six strokes better than two-time Master's champion Bernhard Langer did. The difference? One and one half strokes per day better than Langer does. The Slight Edge.

And it's not just in sports. It's in everything.

In 1998, a book called *The Millionaire Next Door,* by Thomas J. Stanley and William D. Danko, became a runaway best-seller. What so amazed readers was the fact the people profiled in the book were incredibly ordinary, everyday sorts of folks, with normal and even mediocre-level jobs, who had created extraordinary wealth by a truly remarkable, unexpected, amazing strategy. It consisted of—you guessed it. Doing little, mundane, ordinary, insignificant, everyday things with their money.

If you had followed any of those people around for the twenty or thirty or forty years during which they were amassing their financial empires, I promise you, it would not have been breathtakingly exciting—no more exciting than it would be to follow an Olympic athlete in training every day from his 3:30 A.M. wake-up call to his exhausted collapse into bed at night.

We love rags-to-riches stories and underdog-becomes-hero stories, and we use them to motivate people because they are so exciting and dramatic ... aren't they?

Actually, no. The truth is, they're not exciting at all—when they're really happening. They only seem dramatic in the retelling. But the reality is that the rags-to-riches success story person has gotten to where he is by making mundane, quiet, little Slight Edge decisions and repeating simple disciplines, day in and day out.

It's not exciting to read about; it's not exciting to make a movie about. It's not even exciting to do.

But believe me, it sure is exciting when you finally get to experience the results.

No matter in what arena in life or work or play—the difference between winning and losing, the gap that separates success and failure, is so slight, so subtle, most never see it.

Superman may leap tall buildings at a single bound. Here on earth, we win through the Slight Edge.

CHAPTER 6

Two Life Paths

Two roads diverged in a yellow wood
And sorry I could not travel both
And be one traveler, long I stood
And looked down one as far as I could
To where it bent in the undergrowth.

Then took the other as just as fair
And having perhaps the better claim
Because it was grassy and wanted wear
Though as for that, the passing there
Had worn them really about the same.

And both that morning equally lay
In leaves no step had trodden black
Oh, I kept the first for another day!
Yet, knowing how way leads onto way
I doubted if I should ever come back.

I shall be telling this with a sigh
Somewhere ages and ages hence
Two roads diverged in a wood
And I took the one less traveled by
And that has made all the difference.
— Robert Frost, *The Road Not Taken*

There was a time when the people of the world were convinced the sun revolved around the Earth. A few visionaries stubbornly refused to accept what was obvious to everyone else, and because

Copernicus, Galileo and a handful of others risked their lives to chose the road less traveled, the rest of the world eventually caught on to what is now obvious to everyone in the twenty-first century: the Earth revolves around the sun.

What's more, in the last hundred years, we've discovered that even space is curved (though that one's still a little hard for most people to wrap their minds around).

The truth is, *everything* is curved. There is no true straight line; everything is changing—including your life.

You are on a journey, your life path. That path is a curve.

You're curving either upward or downward.

It may seem to you that today was much like yesterday. It wasn't. It was different. Every day is. Appearances can be deceiving—and almost always are. There may be times when things seem to be on a steady, even keel. This is an illusion: in life, there is no such thing as staying in the same place. There are no straight lines; everything curves. If you're not increasing, you're decreasing.

Above and Below the Slight Edge

Let's take a look at what the Slight Edge actually looks like by going back to the wealthy man's lesson. If you make a graph of the penny doubled every day for a month, it will look something like this:

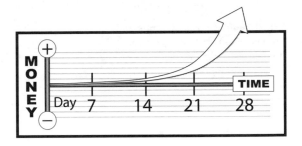

This is not only a picture of compound interest; it's also a picture of how the Slight Edge looks when it's working *for* you.

Now, let's get a sense of what the Slight Edge looks like and feels like when it's working *against* you instead. It's simple: just put a mirror up to the first illustration. This graph shows you that when it's not working in your favor, the Slight Edge can be a very sharp and unforgiving edge indeed!

If you understand and live by the law of compound interest,

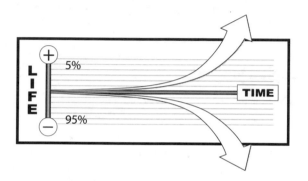

your life will look like the upper half of this graph. If you don't understand and live by the law of compound interest, your life will look like the lower half of this graph.

Wherever you may be in your own life, understanding the Slight Edge will gives you the tools to start fresh—right now!—and place yourself firmly on the upper curve.

The upper curve is the formula for success: a few simple disciplines, repeated every day. The lower curve is the formula for failure: a few simple errors in judgment, repeated every day.

The upper curve represents that one person out of twenty, the five percent who are successful and happy at the end of their lives. The lower curve represents the other nineteen, the ninety-five percent who reach their "golden years" angry and bitter, and have no idea or concept of how they got there or why. Life, it seems to them, is unfair, and that's just how it is. But you and I know that's not the case. It's not a matter of being fair or unfair: it's pure geometry, the geometry of time.

Most people hold time as their enemy; they seek to avoid the passage of time and strive to have results *now*. That's a choice based on a philosophy. Successful people understand that time is their friend. In every choice I make, every course of action I take, I always have time in mind: time is my ally. That, too, is a choice based on a philosophy.

Time will be your friend or your enemy; it will promote you or expose you. It depends purely upon which side of this curve you decide to ride. It's entirely up to you.

If you're doing the simple disciplines, time will promote you. If you're doing the few simple errors in judgment, time will expose you—no matter how well you appear to be doing right now. Time is the great equalizer.

Why People Don't Fly

> If God had meant man to fly, he would have given him wings.
> — Bishop Milton Wright

Have you ever wondered why people can't fly?

We have a phrase we use when something difficult, painful or tragic happens; we say, "Whoa: that's heavy." And indeed, it is. Life is heavy. The predominant force on Earth is gravity, and gravity is always pulling you down.

Just ask Bishop Milton Wright, the founder of Huntingdon College in Huntingdon, Indiana, who is reputed to have pointed out the self-evident truth in the quote above during a sermon he delivered in 1890.

Some people, though, just can't seem to accept self-evident truths. Like two of Bishop Wright's sons, who thirteen years later built and flew the first successful, man-powered, heavier-than-air flying machine. Their names were Wilbur and Orville.

Social science research says that as a child, you heard the word "No" about 40,000 times by the age of five—before you even started first grade. How many times had you heard the word "Yes"? About 5,000. That's eight times as many no's as yes's. Eight times the force holding you down, compared to the force lifting you up. Eight times the gravity against your desire to soar.

Don't do that! Don't say that to your grandmother! Don't slouch! Don't touch that, it's hot! Don't talk to strangers! Don't cross the street! No ... No ... No ...

Mind you, most of these no's are well intended; like the police force motto, their purpose is only to protect and serve. So I'm not criticizing the no's. But where are the yes's?

Author Jerry Wilson, in his landmark 1991 book *Word-of-Mouth Marketing*, based his revolutionary "exceptional customer service" strategy on a statistic he'd found: the average customer will tell three people about a positive experience with a business or product, but will talk about a negative experience to *thirty-three* people! Eleven bad experiences to one positive; eleven reasons an idea won't work to one reason it will.

I mentioned earlier that only about one person out of twenty will ever achieve his or her goals and dreams in life. Regardless of what realm of life or work or play we're talking about, we'll see an average success rate of not more than five percent. Why is that?

Forty thousand no's to five thousand yes's. Thirty-three negatives to every three positives. Is it any wonder that ninety-five percent of us are failing? Is it any wonder most people don't fly?

If you are one of those rare and special five-percenters who decides to ignore gravity and take to the sky—one of those rare birds, like Orville or Wilbur, who chooses to break free of the downward pull of life and rise to a higher quality of life, accomplishment and success, to be a pioneer and risk discomfort and ridicule for the sake of your dreams—well, I've got good news and bad news.

The good news is, you're already exceptionally well oriented toward success.

The bad news is, all those ninety-five others are going to be yanking on you, sitting on you, naysaying and doomsaying on you, and doing their level best to pull you back down. Why? Because if you succeed, you'll make them look as scared and desperate as they're afraid they really are.

If you win, they lose. If you succeed, they fail.

They know instinctively that there are only two ways to make your building the highest building in town: build an even bigger one—or tear down all the others. Since the odds are against most people building the big one, and since it takes just too darn long to start seeing any results, and since they are not at all aware of the Slight Edge, they're taking the path of least resistance, and going into the demolition business.

You can use the Slight Edge to break free of the downward pull of life and become the best you can possibly be. Or, the Slight Edge will pull you down, keep you down, and eventually take you out of your life. It's up to you.

For things to change, *you've* got to change. For things to get better, *you've* got to get better. It's easy to do. But it's easy not to do, too.

Blame and Responsibility

> A man can fail many times, but he isn't a failure until he begins to blame somebody else.
>
> — John Burroughs

If you want to measure where you are, if you want to know whether you're on the success curve or on the failure curve, or if you want to assess anyone else and determine which curve they're on, here's how. There is one attitude, one state of mind, which overwhelmingly predominates either side of the curve.

The predominant state of mind displayed by those people on the failure curve is *blame*. The predominant state of mind displayed by those people on the success curve is *responsibility*.

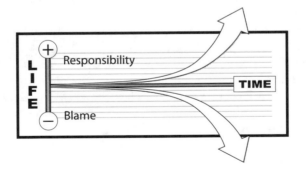

People on the success curve live a life of responsibility. They take full responsibility for who they are, where they are, and everything that happens to them.

Taking responsibility liberates you; in fact, it is perhaps the single most liberating thing there is. Even when it hurts, even when it doesn't seem fair. When you don't take responsibility, when you blame others, circumstances, fate or chance, you give away your power. When you take and retain full responsibility—even when others are wrong or the situation is genuinely unfair—you keep your life's reins in your own hands.

Negative and difficult things happen to all of us; most of them are mostly or completely out of our control. It's how we react, how we view those circumstances and conditions, that makes the difference between success and failure—and that is completely within our control.

The five-percenters who dwell on the upper curve know there are no excuses; they understand and accept the fact that nobody can do it to them, and nobody can do it for them. They live by the axiom, "If it's going to be, it's up to me." They set their own standards—and their standards are high. They realize that their only limitations are self-imposed. They understand that it is not what happens to them that's important, but how they respond to what happens that makes the difference between their failure and success.

They are aware of the Slight Edge and they understand how it operates in their lives.

People on the failure curve are masters of blame; they blame everyone and everything—the economy, the government, the oil crisis, the weather, their neighbors, the rich, the poor, the young, the old, their kids, their parents, their boss, their coworkers, their employees. Life itself.

The inhabitants of the lower curve are life's victims, the great mass of "done-to's." The only way these folks can really make much sense of out life is to conclude, "Life is a bitch—and then you die."

I knew a man whose self-declared philosophy was, "Life is an unpleasant practical joke which occurs somewhere between birth and death." On which side of the curve do you think he was living? Where was he headed? Can you imagine what results that thought, "Life is an unpleasant practical joke," would create when magnified by the water-hyacinth-like force of time?

You know the expression, "Be careful what you wish for—you just might get it"? It's not even a question of what you wish for: be careful what you *think*. Because what you think, multiplied by action plus time, will create what you get.

People on the failure curve are oblivious to the Slight Edge— or, if they are aware of it, they take a position of opposition, as if they their lives were dedicated to proving that it isn't real or doesn't really work.

> Responsibility is declaring oneself as cause in the matter. It is a context from which to live one's life.
>
> Responsibility is not a burden, fault, praise, blame, credit, shame or guilt. All these include judgments and evaluations of good and bad, right and wrong, or better and worse. They are not responsibility ...
>
> Responsibility starts with the willingness to deal with a situation from and with the point of view, whether at the moment realized or not, that you are the source of what you are, what you do and what you have.
>
> It is not "right," or even "true," to declare oneself as "cause" in the matter. It's just empowering. By standing for yourself as cause, "what happens" shifts from "happening to you" to "just happening" and, ultimately, to "happening as a result of your being cause in the matter."
>
> — Werner Erhard

The people on the upper half of the Slight Edge curve are the cause of what happens in their lives. They view all the forces that brought them to this point—God, parents, teachers, childhood, circumstances, you name it—with gratitude and appreciation and without blame. And they view what comes next as *their call.*

Are you your own cause?

The people on the upper curve take full responsibility for all the choices they make in their lives and in their work. Do you? It's easy to do ... and just as easy not to do. And if you don't take full responsibility for your thoughts and actions and circumstances right now, will that kill you today? No ... *but!*

But that simple error in judgment compounded over time will absolutely, positively destroy you.

Successful people do what unsuccessful people are not willing to do: they take full responsibility for how the Slight Edge is working in their lives. Unsuccessful people blame the Slight Edge for their lives not working. Successful people know that they cannot afford that luxury.

Past and Future

Try this experiment: Take a comfortable, seated position and look down at the floor; then, without changing position, take the next five minutes to think about your life. Anything and everything, whatever that means to you, just think about your life.

Go ahead and do that now ...

Now, clear your mind, walk around a minute, then come back and do the second half: Take the same comfortable, seated position, only tilt your head up so you're looking at the ceiling. Spend the next five minutes thinking about your life. Anything and everything, whatever that means to you, just think about your life.

Go ahead and do that now ...

I don't know what results you had, but here's what most people find: when looking down, it's pretty hard not to start thinking about the past. When gazing upward, it's pretty hard not to start thinking about the future.

I can promise you, that morning in the Phoenix airport, every single person I saw rushing around was looking either straight ahead, or down!

People on the failure curve tend to focus on their past—and it pulls them down. People on the success curve focus on their future—and it pulls them up.

People on the success curve don't ignore the past, but they use it as a tool, one of many with which they build their futures. People who live on the failure curve use the past as a weapon with which they bludgeon themselves and the people around them. Regrets, recriminations, remorse and retribution.

A friend of mine says that people make two lists about their spouses and carry these lists around in their heads. The long list is a list of "what's wrong," and they consult that list every day. The short list is a list of "what's right." That's the list they read for the eulogy.

People on the success curve don't wait until the funeral. They burn the long list and spend every day reading from the short list. They make themselves experts in "what's right," and let go of "what's wrong." They never hold a grudge—not because it's morally wrong (although they may agree with that reason, too), but because it gets in the way. It slows them down. They're too busy moving toward the future to be staring into the rear view mirror.

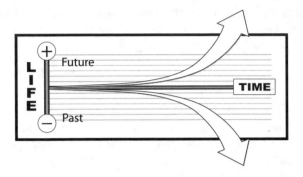

One of the quickest and most direct routes to getting yourself up and onto the success curve is to get out of the past. Review the past, but only for the purpose of making a better plan. Review it, understand and take responsibility for the errors you've made, and use it as a tool to do differently in the future. And don't spend a great deal time doing even that!—the future is a far better tool than the past.

The future is your most powerful tool and your best friend. Devote some serious, focused time and effort into designing a crystal-clear picture of where you're going. In the second part of this book, we'll take a look at specific ways to help you do exactly that. For now, I'll just say this: when you do have a clear picture of the future and consciously put time every day into letting yourself be drawn forward by that future, it will pull you through whatever friction and static you encounter in the present—and whatever tugging and clutching you may feel from the past.

One last thing about past and future—and I *have* saved the best for last.

You can't change the past. You can change the future. Would you rather be influenced by something you can't change, or something you can?

Where Are You Headed?

"Would you tell me please, which way I ought to go from here?"
"That depends a good deal on where you want to go," said the
Cat. "I don't much care where—" said Alice. "Then it doesn't
matter which way you go," said the Cat. "—so long as I get
somewhere," Alice added as an explanation. "Oh, you're sure to
do that," said the Cat, "if you only walk long enough."

— Lewis Carroll, *Alice's Adventures in Wonderland*

On which side of the Slight Edge curve are you standing right
now? Which way are you headed? Are you one of the five-percenters, one of those rare individuals living on the success curve
and going up—or are you among the great majority, the ninety-
five percenters on the failure curve and sliding down?

Not sure? Perhaps, in the middle, you say? Sorry, there is no
middle. You are either going up or going down. The early part of
both curves are fairly flat, so it can certainly look like you're moving along on a nice, even keel, heading neither up nor down. But
appearances can be deceiving. (And usually are.) In a constantly
and rapidly changing world like ours, you simply cannot remain
the same as you were yesterday. You are in motion—you have no
choice in that.

But in which direction? You have total choice in that.

You are either improving or diminishing in personal and professional value. Your relationships are growing deeper and richer,
or growing more stale and distant. You are learning more and
more about the truths of life, or slipping deeper and deeper into
denial about the truths of life. You are building your long-term
security and financial freedom, or dismantling it. And your health
is building day by day ... or ebbing slowly away.

There is no treading water in life, no running in place,
because everything is in motion. If you're not improving, enriching, building, unfolding, if you're not adding assets to your personal and professional value every day—then you're headed down
the curve.

So, let's take an honest look at your life. Where are you right
now?

Let's take an honest look at your health.
Are you building it every day? The way you eat, the way you

exercise, the kind of schedule you keep, the ways in which you take care of yourself—are all these building a greater feeling of health and vibrancy every day? Or does it feel like you're making more and more withdrawals from your life-energy bank account, and the balance is steadily decreasing?

Is your health on the success curve or failure curve?

Let's take an honest look at your personal development.

Are you learning more about yourself, about the world around you, and about how life works every day? Are you learning new skills and sharpening old ones? Are you becoming a more capable person, one more interesting to know and valuable to be around? Or is your character being gradually etched with the age-lines of disappointment, disillusionment, boredom and bitterness?

Is your personal development on the success curve or the failure curve?

Let's take an honest look at your relationships.

Is the number of friends in your life, people with whom you stay in touch, with whom you share meaningful exchanges and mutually enriching experiences, growing larger every year? If you are married, and you were to describe your marriage as a plant, would it be a plant that is growing taller, riper, fuller and richer with each passing year? What about your family—children, parents, brothers, sisters and others? Are they growing deeper and richer or more distant and shallower?

Are your relationships on the success curve or the failure curve?

Let's take an honest look at your finances.

Are you building assets and putting money into a long-term plan that will create true financial freedom? Is your net worth growing larger each year?

Are you living within your means and investing a portion of your income into a program that will build equity for you over the years, growing dollar by dollar and picking up momentum through the power of compounding interest so that, like a snowball rolling down a wintry hill, it will have gathered tremendous financial mass in the years when you need it most?

Or are you living on credit, on borrowed money as well as borrowed time, running your coffers empty and storing up debt instead of equity, digging yourself deeper and deeper into a hole that grows only harder to escape?

Are your finances on the success curve or the failure curve?

Let's take an honest look at your life itself.

What kind of impact is your life having on the world around you? How is the world different as a result of your being here? After you leave this world, what will you leave behind as a legacy and how will people remember you? When you add together your career and all your professional accomplishments, your relationships and all your personal accomplishments, your sense of connection with nature, humanity and God, how would you describe the overall value or meaning of your life? And is that sense growing stronger, deeper, richer, more powerful every day, month and year?

Is your life on the success curve or the failure curve?

Be honest about all of this. Do as Shakespeare's Polonius tells his son Laertes to do:

This above all, to thine own self be true; and it must follow, as the night the day, thou canst not then be false to any man.

— William Shakespeare, *Hamlet, Act 1, Scene 3*

If you don't tell the truth about where you really are in your life—right now—then you're cheating yourself out of an extraordinary opportunity. Because right now, this very minute, can be the time you look back on as the moment your life changed for the better—forever!

Life is not a practice session; there's no dress rehearsal. This is it. This is for real. So, play straight and true with yourself. Take a look at your life and tell the truth about where you're really at.

Do this exercise with me right now. Take a pencil (not a pen—remember, everything changes) and put a check in the UP or DOWN box next to each area of your life as listed below. Which way are you going?

	UP	DOWN
Your health	____	____
Your personal development	____	____
Your relationships	____	____
Your finances	____	____
Your life itself	____	____

Where are you? Which side of the line do you fall on in each area of your life?

If you have more "down" checks than "up," I have two things to say: the first is thank you for being honest! And the second is, don't worry, you're not alone. Remember, gravity has been pulling you down since day 1. Remember that you've heard eight no's for every yes, and eleven negative comments for every positive one! And those no's and negatives are compounding with the force of the water hyacinth, threatening to cover the surface of your mind with a suffocating weed that blots out all possibility of sunlight reaching the life that's wanting to thrive there. The one or two "no's" didn't kill you—but those 40,000 can sure do some serious damage to your sense of possibility.

That's the Slight Edge working against you.

The Good News

Now, here's the good news: where you are right now is poised in the present, with the past stretching behind you and the future lying ahead. You cannot change the past. You can absolutely change the future.

Are you heading up, or heading down? Right at this moment, at this exact juncture in your life, you can answer the question either way. At any moment in your life, you can choose to change which side of that curve you're on.

The good news is the wealthy man's third gift: you have a choice.

Where you've been heading is not necessarily where you will be heading after you turn this page, or put down this book, or wake up tomorrow morning. The past does not equal the future.

In fact, you cannot look in both directions at once. You can look down, or you can look up; you can look back, or you can look forward; you can look in the rearview mirror, or at the highway ahead.

Step onto the upper curve, the path of success, and you will put any area of life—your health, your finances, your relationships, your family life, your career, your spiritual health, your sense of accomplishment and fulfillment and purpose—on track within a handful of years at most.

If you don't step onto the upper curve? Failing is something that will take the rest of your life. Failure, unchecked by a choice to change, is a life-long condition.

What matters now is your awareness of how the Slight Edge operates in your life and your understanding that you have what you need right now to change that. All the information you need is already out there—and, right here. You're already doing the actions. All you need to do is choose to have to them serve and empower you—and *keep on choosing*.

In my line of work, I talk a lot about success in financial terms. But genuine success is a far greater issue than purely financial health. A genuinely successful life means your health, your family relationships, your career, your spirituality, your sense of fulfillment, your legacy and the impact you have on the world. It's all these things and more. And the best thing about genuine success is that it spreads! Success in any one of these areas begins to affect all the others, too. Improve your health and you improve your relationships; work on your personal development and you have an impact on your career. Everything affects everything.

Do you have all the skills, knowledge, information, money and health and friends and every other resource you'll need to accomplish everything in your life ... right now? No. Can you put your hands on all those resources right now? No.

But can you make a choice—and come up with one penny?

That's all it takes to start.

PART TWO

Mastering Your Life

CHAPTER 7

Mastering the Slight Edge

It resists definition yet can be instantly recognized. It comes in many variations, yet follows certain unchanging laws. It brings rich rewards, yet it is not really a goal or a destination but rather a process, or journey. We call this journey *mastery* and tend to assume that it requires a special ticket available only to those born with exceptional abilities. But mastery is not reserved for the supertalented or even for those who are fortunate enough to have gotten an early start. It's available to anyone who is willing to get on the path and stay on it—regardless of age, sex or experience.

The trouble is that we have few, if any, maps to guide us on the journey or even to show us how to find the path. The modern world, in fact, can be viewed as a prodigious conspiracy against mastery. We're continually bombarded with promises of immediate gratification, instant success, and fast, temporary relief, all of which lead in exactly the wrong direction ...

— George Leonard, *Mastery*

Mastery is not some vaulted, lofty place that only the elite few ever land. The pursuit of any aim, goal or dream—personal, professional, spiritual, in any area—is a Slight Edge journey of continuous improvement, learning and refinement. But mastery is not an exalted state that lies at the end of the path; it is a state of mind that lies at the very beginning. According to George Leonard, author of *Education* and *Ecstasy and The Way of Aikido*, mastery is the act of setting your foot on the path.

As a fifth *dan* black belt in Aikido and award-winning writer on education, fitness and personal development, Leonard has more than a passing acquaintance with mastery, and what this master has to say about the subject is remarkably liberating.

There are no shortcuts, he says, no special tickets needed, and none available even if you wanted one. You don't need to be born with exceptional abilities to enter into mastery, nor is it reserved for the super-talented. You don't even need to have gotten an early start.

The upward journey of success on the Slight Edge curve is available to anyone who is willing to get on the path and stay on it. But it's only by being immersed in the process, the day-by-day progression, that you will come to know the road. That's how you will acquire and refine the skills and awareness you'll need to master the Slight Edge and, therefore, master your success and your life.

All that's required is taking the first step.

Baby Steps

When you were a tiny child, you made your way around your world on your hands and knees crawling. Everyone around you was walking, and one day you got it into your little head that maybe you could give that a try. And once you had that thought, you *had* to give it a try. It was simply the next frontier; there was no way you weren't going to master it.

So, step by step—literally!—you worked on developing the skills you needed to walk.

You grabbed onto something above you and pulled yourself upright. You stood up, holding on to a playpen or chair or some big stuffed animal. You were wobbly and unsure. You let go, either on purpose or by accident, and it didn't matter which, because the result was the same—*Crash!* You fell down. And then, either right away, or later that day, or the next day (and it didn't matter when), you tried it again. And then you tried it again, and again ... until eventually, you stood up all by yourself—no hands.

Then you took a step—and in that step, according to George Leonard, you assumed the mantle of mastery ... even if external appearances didn't entirely confirm your new status. (Remember, appearances can be deceiving—and almost always are.)

So here you are, just completing your very first step. Now, you know that the big people you've been watching go around taking one step after another. You've watched them do it: right foot, left foot, right foot, left ... so you try. You complete that first, tentative, epic-making step and get ready to swing into the next one—and then, *Crash!*

Try again. And again. And again. After days of side-stepping around the coffee table, awkwardly bringing one little foot out from behind the other while you hold onto Mom's or Dad's fingers, you eventually take your first sequence of *two* steps ... then three, and four, and ... all alone ... all by yourself ... and to the encouraging cheers and applause of your proud family—baby steps ... one at a time ... *and you're walking!*

In the process of learning to walk, did you spend more time falling down or standing up? If you were anything like most babies, you failed (fell) far more than you succeeded (walked). Didn't matter: you were on the path of mastery.

Did you ever have the thought of quitting? Did you ever say to yourself, *You know, it looks like maybe I'm just not cut out for walking ... oh well. I guess I'll just have to crawl for the rest of my life—which really isn't all that bad, when you stop and think about it. I'm sure I'll get used to it ... ?* Of course not. You were on the path of mastery. You were already a master—now it was only a matter of your walking skills catching up.

Constantly falling down was really uncomfortable—it hurt!— and you probably looked pretty silly lying there on the floor like a beetle on its back ... but you kept at it anyway. Why? Because successful people do what unsuccessful people are not willing to do—and *all babies are successful.* All babies are masters; we're designed that way. All babies instinctively understand the Slight Edge. We only let go of our natural pull towards success, our mastery, over the course of those 40,000 no's.

Are there any situations in your life today where you've given up and decided to keep crawling rather than go for what you really want, what you truly deserve? Have you lost the ability to make up a goal, go for it and get it? Why don't you do what you did when you were just a year old?

The answer is both simple and sad: somewhere along the way, you lost faith. You became too grown-up to take baby steps, too sure you would never succeed to let yourself fail a few times first. You gave up on the universal truth that simple little disciplines, done again and again over time, would move the biggest mountains.

You forgot what you used to know about the Slight Edge. You stepped off the path of mastery.

There is something treacherous about letting go of that child-like willingness to try and try again. Something insidiously dangerous about buying into the idea, "that'll never work for me." It is this: settling for less, settling for failure and giving up on baby steps soon becomes a habit. The first time you give up, it's painful. But the more you give up, the easier and easier it gets—and success recedes further and further from your grasp.

Can you guess why? That's right: it's the Slight Edge—working against you. Life is heavy ... welcome to the ninety-five percent!

But as always, all we need to do is turn the coin over to find the good news here: it is *just as easy* to step into the habit of succeeding, as it is to slip into the habit of failing. The longer you live, the easier it can get.

And you can step back onto the path of mastery any time you want.

Wanting

> There is one quality which one must possess to win, and that is definiteness of purpose, the knowledge of what one wants, and a burning desire to possess it.
>
> — Napoleon Hill, *Think and Grow Rich*

We all have visions of the way we'd like things to be that are different from the way they are. It could be something as simple as wishing we weighed ten pounds less, or something as far-reaching as wishing we could feed the millions of children around the world who go to bed hungry every night.

When I sat having my shoes polished in the Phoenix airport, I couldn't have stopped myself from having a vision of the shoeshine woman's success if I'd tried. I *wanted* her to be successful, so much that it ached.

It's that ache that we need look at now for a moment, the ache of *wanting*.

Having a dream is not always a matter of all roses and sweetness; ambitions, aspirations and desires can be uncomfortable, even painful.

The word "want" has two meanings. It can mean you desire something; it can also mean you lack something. And in a way, those aren't really two meanings; they're two sides of the same meaning. We tend to desire what we lack, and lack what we desire.

That means your dreams can be painful. Letting yourself become aware of what it is that you desire, but do not presently have, means experiencing the "lack" side of the coin as well as the "desire" side. It means becoming more fully aware of what you don't have. It means staring at your present reality with a sober eye and refusing to kid yourself. And noticing that you're not where you want to be can be uncomfortable.

Wanting hurts.

Here's an interesting thing: if putting voice to your fondest dreams can make you a little uncomfortable, it can also make everyone around you uncomfortable, and often far more so. Tell your five closest friends about your biggest ambition, and watch how many of them squirm! Why? Because showing them your want (desire) also reminds them of their want (lack).

This is one reason that when you are formulating goals and creating a vision for your future, it's important to be careful whom you share them with. It's natural to share your enthusiasm with everyone around you—and it's also useful to remember that people often tend to respond by raining on your parade. When they do, it's not out of malice or the conscious desire to blunt your excitement. More often, it's simply a form of self-defense. They'd rather not hear about the vision you have, because it reminds them of the one they've lost.

Closing the Gap

When you took an honest look at your life back in the previous chapter, rating yourself as being on the success curve or failure curve in different areas, you were painting a picture of where you are *now*. The diagram shows that as point A, and where you *could be*, your vision of what's possible for you in your life, as point B.

To the extent that there is a gap between points A and B, there is a natural tension between those two, like holding a magnet near a piece of iron. You can feel the magnet tugging at the iron—and you can feel your dreams (B) tugging at your present circumstances (A).

"Where I Am"   "Where I Could Be"

A   B

Tension is uncomfortable. That's why it sometimes makes people uncomfortable to hear about how things *could be*. One of the reasons Dr. Martin Luther King, Jr.'s famous "I have a dream" speech made such a huge impact on the world and carved such a vivid place in our cultural memory is that it made the world of August 1963 very uncomfortable. John Lennon sang his vision of a more peaceful world in the song "Imagine"; within the decade, he was shot to death. Visions and visionaries make people uncomfortable.

These are of course especially dramatic examples, but the same principle applies to the personal dreams and goals of people we've never heard of. The same principle applies to everyone, including you and me.

Let's say you have a brother, or sister or old friend, with whom you had a falling out years ago. You wish you had a better relationship, that you talked more often, that you shared more personal experiences and conversations together. Between where you are today, and where you can imagine being, there is a gap. Can you feel it?

Or let's say you are a hard worker and make a pretty good income, but have no solid retirement plan and don't know how you'll be able to live comfortably when you reach your late sixties. There's how you'd *like* to be living at age sixty-eight, and how you're worried you *may end up* living at age sixty-eight if things go the way they're going. Between those two, there's a gap. Can you feel it?

Do you have any health or fitness goals? Career goals? Goals for your kids? Dreams of living somewhere else, of doing something else? Each of those images you have, of how things *could be* but at the moment are *not*, creates a gap with your present reality.

Most people, when confronted by problems larger than or of a different sort than they're already handling, immediately feel defeated or thrown off course. Most tend to see larger or different problems as negatives, and infect their own lives with negativity. What they don't realize is this philosophy: *The size of the problem determines the size of the person.*

You can gauge the limitations of a person's life by the size of the problems that get him or her down. You can measure the impact a person's life has by the size of the problems he or she solves.

If the size of the problems you solve is, "I put the cans in the bottom of the bag, and put the bread on top," as a grocery store bagger, that's the level of your problem solving and that's the level of your pay. If you can solve big problems, you can graduate to big pay—because the size of your income will be determined by the size of the problems you solve, too!

What most people call a "problem" is simply a gap, an open space between point A and point B. And if you keep an open mind, it's an open space you can bridge.

Now, here is the reason I've spent time describing and explaining this gap: *That gap can work against you or it can work for you.*

The gap between A and B cannot last forever. It has to resolve, and it will, one way or the other. It's a law of nature, and there's nothing you can do to stop it. But you do have a choice in how it resolves.

One way to resolve the tension is to move your point A (the way things are today) steadily closer and closer to point B. Let yourself be drawn by the magnet of your dreams, pulled along by the future. Remember what pulls those who dwell in the failure curve? The past. And what pulls people who live on the success curve? The future.

People who live with huge, vivid, clearly articulated dreams are pulled along towards those dreams with such force, they become practically unstoppable. What made people like Martin Luther King, Jr., Gandhi or Mother Teresa, Edison or IBM's Thomas Watson, Wilberforce or Lincoln such forces of nature that nothing could stand in their way, no matter what the odds or obstacles? It was not some magic in their character, though they certainly became people of unusual character along the way. It was the power of their dreams. The vision each of these men and women held created a magnetic force against which no opposition could stand.

Again, I'm using dramatic examples of famous people, but the exact same thing occurs with people you and I have never heard of, everyday people who are not at all famous, but simply have dreams they care about and keep alive every day. That's the force you can harness in the pursuit of your own dreams.

What about the other direction? I said there were two ways that tension can resolve, and the other way is the one that works against you. If you don't close the gap by moving your present circumstance (A) constantly towards your goals and dreams (B), how else can you let the tension resolve?

Quit dreaming.

Just let go of all your dreams, goals, ambitions and aspirations. Settle for less. Make point B disappear, just delete it, and— *poof!*—the tension is gone. And that, sadly, is the choice that the ninety-five percent who travel the failure curve eventually make.

It's not hard to understand why so many people make that second choice. After all, when you're standing here at point A, gazing off into the distance at point B, it's easy to be intimidated by how far away it looks. People don't even want to set foot on the path if they don't think they can make it to the end. *Why even try? I mean, if the mountain's that huge, why take the first step? I'll probably never make it anyway ...* When the journey seems daunting, "easy not to do" can be a lot more appealing than "easy to do"!

But remember, you have to go one direction or the other; you can't stand still. Everything is constantly changing. There are only two possibilities. Either you let go of where you are and get to where you could be, or you hang onto where you are and give up where you could be. You are either going for your dreams or giving up your dreams. Stretching for what you could be, or settling for what you are. There is simply no in-between. Remember, this is the Slight Edge—and doing nothing means going down.

It's your choice.

The Deceptive Majority

> All truth passes through three stages. First, it is ridiculed.
> Second, it is violently opposed. Third, it is accepted as being
> self-evident.
>
> — Arthur Schopenhauer

Those two Slight Edge curves, the success curve and the failure
curve, run parallel to each other for a long time. The two paths
may be so close together that it's almost impossible for most people even to see the distinction between them. Then, all of a sudden, they veer away from each other, the success curve shooting
up like an eagle and the failure curve plummeting downward like
a stock market crash.

The people living on top, who take responsibility, live a life
that is in some ways uncomfortable. Successful people do what
unsuccessful people are not willing to do, and that often means
living outside the limits of one's comfort zone. When you're one
out of twenty, you're always going to be going the opposite direction from the other nineteen.

The people on the other side are comfortable; they're with
the masses. Their lives are more comfortable early on—but
become more uncomfortable later on. Suddenly, late in life, they
find they don't have the finances, don't have the health, no longer
have the relationships, and their lives become very uncomfortable.

Those on the success curve, by contrast, end up far more
comfortable later on, because they have the finances, the health,
the relationships, the successes.

This means changing your thinking about the comfort zone.
It's a change in philosophy. It means embracing living uncomfort-
ably in order to attain a life that is genuinely comfortable—not
deceptively comfortable.

The wonderful quote from Schopenhauer (above) is a brilliant insight to the nature of the majority. The majority always let
the first and second phases pass them by and wait until a truth is
self-evident before signing on. What Schopenhauer is saying is
the key to success is to identify things that are going to become
self-evident *before* they're self-evident! Or to put it even more simply: find out what the majority is doing and do the opposite.

Of course, you have to apply some intelligence; you can't

expect things to work just because they're in opposition to the majority. But the chances are excellent that when you step up onto the success curve, you will be stepping out alone. Like Wilberforce, Edison, Lincoln and Gandhi.

Do the opposite of the majority. Risk being the one, not one of the nineteen. Will people criticize you? Of course. But have you ever seen a statue erected for a critic? We don't build statues for the ninety-five percent: we build them for the five percent.

What I Learned from My Own Funeral

At one point in my life, I entered the corporate world and went to work for Texas Instruments. I was all ready to work my way up in management, but life had other plans for me. I showed up for work and they put me in sales.

I was horrified. I didn't want to be a salesperson. I hated sales. I didn't think I could do it. I *knew* I couldn't do it. What I had was not fear of rejection; it was *terror* of rejection. I knew what I would do—I would quit this job and go back to graduate school.

But successful people do what unsuccessful people are not willing to do. I was up against the wall: I *had* to do it and I knew it.

For my first sales call, I pored through the customer files and found the tiniest, most insignificant account I could: a tiny little drug store in Gainesville, Florida. I figured that if I was going to make a mess, I might as well do as little damage as possible.

I drove for two and a half hours to arrive at that store, white-knuckled with fear. I parked and sat in the lot for a good half hour, leaning my face into the air conditioner vents (with the AC turned up full blast) and sweating buckets. I was terrified. Staying in that car would have been the easiest thing in the world to do right then. And on some level, even though I had not yet articulated the Slight Edge philosophy in my life, I knew that this simple little error, compounded over time, would rob me of all my dreams.

As I had prepared myself to go on this first sales call, I had been literally praying for help, and as so often happens when you ask a question in all sincerity, an answer came. In this case, it came in the form of an article I happened to read in a magazine.

The article was about funerals, and it informed me that at the average funeral, about ten people cry.

I couldn't believe it. *Ten people? That's it? You mean, I go through my entire life, spend years and years going through all these trials and tribulations and achievements and joys and heartbreaks—and at the end of it, there are only ten people who care enough to cry?*

I went on to the next paragraph. It got worse.

Once those ten (or fewer) people had yanked their hankies and honked their noses, the article told me, and my funeral was over, the number one factor that would determine how many people would go on from the funeral to attend the actual burial would be ... the weather. (The weather?!) If it happened to be raining, it said, fifty percent of the people who attend my funeral would decide not to go to my burial after all.

I really couldn't believe it. *You mean, I'm lying there, at the grand conclusion of everything I've ever said and done, of everything I call my life, in those final moments when my entire life is called to account and acknowledged and memorialized by those nearest and dearest to me, those whose lives I've most deeply and profoundly touched ... and half the congregation checks out halfway through because of the weather?!*

At first, this really bummed me out.

And then, it was liberating.

You know what? I thought. *I don't give a damn what anybody thinks of what I'm doing any more. If the odds are that iffy as to whether or not they even cry at my funeral, and chances are fifty-fifty that they duck out anyway before I'm planted if the sky happens to cry for me more than the people do ... then why am I spending so much time worrying about what they're thinking now?*

Why would I be afraid of rejection? Why would I be concerned about what the majority thinks? Why would I be worried about what the ninety-five percent say, think, or do?

Facing some truths about one's own death can also bring one face to face with some important truths about one's life. Reading that article enlarged my comfort zone, and gave me an edge of courage—just a tiny edge, but an edge I hadn't had before. A Slight Edge.

I finally mustered what courage I could, turned off the car, went inside and gave what I am convinced to this day was the worst presentation in the history of sales. They did not buy a thing. In that sense, it was a total failure—but when I got back in my car, I was elated. I had blown the sales call, and achieved a victory in my life.

A few days later, I happened to be thinking about that article as I sat in my car, stopped in traffic. Just then, I saw why we were all stopped: a funeral procession went by. It took less than a minute because it contained only a few cars.

As traffic slowly started moving again, I thought, *That person lived his or her entire life worrying about what other people thought ...*

And it suddenly hit me. Who has long funeral processions? At whose funerals do thousands cry? For whom do the millions mourn? For those who will do what others are not willing to do. For the people for whom we erect statues.

Martin Luther King, Jr., Gandhi, Mother Teresa, Lincoln.

Gigantic funerals are held and great crowds, sometimes entire nations, mourn for those people who spent their lives not worrying about what others thought.

CHAPTER 8

Faces of the Slight Edge

The highest good is like water.

Water gives life to the ten thousand things and yet does not compete with them.

It flows in places that the mass of people detest and therefore is it close to the Way.

— Lao Tzu, *Tao Te Ching*

The Slight Edge is simple and constant. At the same time, the more you understand it and the more you become familiar with it, the more you will come to recognize its influence in your life in many forms and under many disguises.

It is the irresistible force delivered by the tidal wash that polishes the sharp edges of a rocky reef to porcelain smoothness; it is as ever-present in all aspects of life as the water molecule is in biology.

It is the force hiding within the music that "soothes the savage breast." Writing about love, the Apostle Paul said that it is a force that "endures all things and conquers all things," and within the universal human solvent of love, it's not hard to recognize the power of the Slight Edge. Mark Twain wrote, "Against the assault of laughter, nothing can stand." That is the power of the Slight Edge.

There are several faces of the Slight Edge I want to point out to you because they each represent a power that, once you recognize it in your life, you can harness in your pursuit of your dreams.

They are momentum; completion; habit; reflection; and celebration.

Harness the Power of Momentum

Who won the race—the tortoise or the hare? We all know the answer to that one. Yet we live in a world where most everyone has come to expect instant this and instant that, and if we don't get the results we're after fast and faster, we quit.

Get rich quick. The fast lane. That fellow standing in front of the microwave muttering, "Hurry uppp, hurry uppp ... " Fast, faster, fastest is a strategy that will eventually take you *down* the Slight Edge curve.

M.I.T. professor Peter Senge puts this beautifully in his bestselling business book, *The Fifth Discipline—The Art & Practice of the Learning Organization:*

> Virtually all natural systems, from ecosystems to animals to organizations, have intrinsically optimal rates of growth. The optimal rate is far less than the fastest possible growth. When growth becomes excessive—as it does in cancer—the system itself will seek to compensate by slowing down; perhaps putting the organization's survival at risk in the process.
> — Peter Senge, *The Fifth Discipline*

Have you ever witnessed something or someone that grew too fast? A business that expanded too rapidly and then self-destructed? A rock star, movie star or sports star who became a shooting star and went BOA—Burned Out on Arrival? Faster can end up being slower; too fast often puts the system's (or the person's) survival at risk.

Dr. Senge talks about "intrinsically optimal rates of growth"; your optimal rate of growth is always served best by a step-by-step approach of constant, never-ending improvement, which lays solid foundations and builds upon them over and over. The Slight Edge is your optimal rate of growth. Simple disciplines compounded over time. That's how the tortoise won; that's how you get to be a winner, too.

Having said that let me ask this: What is the real point of the story of the tortoise and the hare? Altogether now: *Slow and steady wins the race, right?* But notice something here: the point is not that there's any special virtue to moving slowly. There's nothing inherently good about slowness, and it's just as possible to move too slowly as to move too quickly.

The key word in the Aesop moral is not "slow"—it's *steady*. Steady wins the race. That's the truth of it.

The fable of the tortoise and the hare is really about the remarkable power of momentum. A body at rest tends to stay at rest—and a body in motion tends to remain in motion. That's why your activity is so important. Once you're in motion, it's easy to keep on keeping on. Once you stop, it's hard to change from stop to go.

> Be not afraid of going slowly; be afraid only of standing still.
>
> — Chinese proverb

In my business, I coach people how to build large organizations one person at a time, by doing very simple, easy-to-do actions every day. I've found that it's far more effective to take one business-building action every day for a week, than to take seven, or ten, or even two dozen, all at once and then take the rest of the week off. People who do the first, week in and week out, build an organization; people who do the second, don't—*even if they actually take a greater number of those business-building actions than the other people.*

Why not? No momentum. After six days off, they have to start all over again, getting themselves geared up and inspired to get back into action. It can take a good amount of energy and initiative to get yourself started in a new activity—but it takes far, far less to keep yourself doing it once you've started.

There's another reason once a day is better than seven times, once a week: the daily rhythm of the thing starts to change you. It becomes part of your routine, and as it does, it becomes part of who you are. That doesn't happen with a once-in-a-while, all-out effort.

Imagine taking a twenty-minute brisk walk in the morning, and then in the late afternoon, working out on a home gym for another twenty minutes. Now imagine that for a week, you did that every day. How would you feel at the end of the week?

Now instead, what if on that first day you had taken a 140-minute walk (that's over two hours!) and that afternoon, spent another 140 minutes on the home gym—and then done nothing for the next six days?

Steady wins the race.

When you're in motion, it's also far easier to make positive changes in your direction. It's like steering a car: when the car's sitting still, moving the wheel is hard work, but when it's moving, even at only 10 or 20 mph, turning is a breeze. It's a breeze because you're *already in the flow.*

The Slight Edge is a flow, and it moves at its own pace, automatically homing in on optimal growth rates. Part of understanding the Slight Edge is learning to go with the flow. You can be as impatient as you like, but it won't bother the Slight Edge. It's always moving at its own optimal speed, with or without your consent, whether you are aware of it moving or not.

To make the most of the Slight Edge flow, you'll want to match the speed of your growth and development to the natural progression of the Slight Edge. That's accomplished naturally by having a Slight Edge strategy.

It's easy to stay active. It's also easy not to. And if you stop, it won't kill you today—*but*, that simple error in judgment, compounded over time, will absolutely destroy the getting of any goal you're after.

Mary Kay Ash put this simply: *"Give yourself something to work toward—constantly."*

Harness the Power of Completion

Another way you gather momentum and harness it to your advantage is by practicing an activity called *completion*.

Are there any things that are incomplete in your life? Any unpaid bills? Have you done your taxes? Did you borrow a book or tool you have yet to return? Is there someone who needs to hear you say, "I love you," or, "I'm sorry," or, "Thank you—I appreciate you"? Do you have any unfinished projects? Any unkept promises—taking a weekend away with your spouse, or taking your kids somewhere special? Are there any agreements or commitments you've left hanging?

Each and every incomplete thing in your life or work exerts a draining force on you, sucking the energy of accomplishment and success out of you as surely as a vampire stealing your blood.

Every incomplete promise, commitment and agreement saps your strength, because it blocks your momentum, inhibits your ability to move forward, to progress and improve. Incomplete things keep calling you back to the past to take care of them.

Here's the unfortunate and powerfully destructive truth of being incomplete: it keeps the past alive. Remember, people who live on the success curve are pulled by the future, while those who dwell on the failure curve are pulled by the past. And a surefire way to be forced to live as a prisoner of your past is not to complete things.

Is it easy to do? Yes ... —wait. Let's consider that for a moment. No ... actually, it's *not* always easy to complete those incomplete things in life. Not when you've got a truckload of them to take care of. That stack of incompletions can loom larger than the Sears Tower. They can be absolutely overwhelming. Especially when you realize that whatever might have been keeping you from completing them in the first place—fear of confronting the issue, feeling intimidated or overwhelmed by it, worrying it might be difficult or uncomfortable—well, that's been compounded by the Slight Edge, too!

That's the Slight Edge working against you. That's how the pile got so big to begin with. And the truth is even those incompletions that seem difficult to do would have been a lot easier to do them when they first came up than they might be now.

Approaching that stack of undones with the Slight Edge in hand is not only the best way to deal with them, it's the *only* way you'll ever deal with them. Take on those incompletions in your life just as you took on learning to walk. Baby steps, one at a time, letting the Slight Edge work for you to help you complete whatever needs completing.

Take on any one of your "incomplete" projects, one at a time. And if even that one project seems like too huge a mountain to climb, rummage around its foothills until you find an initial step you can take. The biggest meal is still eaten one bite at a time. Think of the title of Art Williams' bestseller, *All You Can Do Is All You Can Do, But All You Can Do Is Enough.* So find something you can do, and do that.

Make a phone call. Write a letter. Give fifteen minutes to completing something every day.

Is it easy not to do? Absolutely. And if you don't do it today, will it destroy you? (You know the rest, so sing along ...)

Each time you do complete something, you get to move on with your luggage a little lighter and a bit more spring in your step.

Harness the Power of Habit

> Sow an act, reap a habit;
> Sow a habit, reap a character;
> Sow a character, reap a destiny.
>   — Anonymous (attributed to various)

We often take habits for granted. There are bad habits you try to break but can't, good habits you wish you had but don't, annoying habits others have you wish they didn't, and odd habits you picked up yourself somewhere, for reasons totally mysterious to you. We're all aware that habits exist, though we often are not as aware of our own as others are.

However, we seldom realize the enormous power of habits.

There are two kinds of habits: those that serve you, and those that don't. Brushing your teeth is a habit that serves you; biting your nails is one that doesn't. Thinking things through for yourself serves you; blindly accepting everything you read on the Internet or hear on television doesn't. Looking for the best in people serves you; anticipating their worst doesn't.

The first type of habit wields the force of the Slight Edge on your behalf and moves you along the success curve; the second turns the Slight Edge subtly but remorselessly against you and pulls you down the failure curve.

A habit is something you do without thinking. You come home from work, walk into the house, pull a beer out of the fridge and flick on the TV while you're talking to someone on the phone, without any conscious decision that a beer is exactly what you need right now or that there is something you urgently need to see on television.

Getting up early can become a habit. So can getting up late and staying up late. Complaining can become a habit. Spending more than you earn can become a habit; so can putting a piece of every paycheck into a retirement account. Looking for the positive side of every challenge can become a habit, so can finding the cloud in every silver lining.

The way a behavior turns into a habit is by repeating it over and over and over again until it becomes automatic. The creation of habits is a pure Slight Edge: simple little actions, repeated over time. The compounded effect of those habits over time will work either for you or against you, depending on whether they're habits that serve you, or habits that don't.

Your habits are what will propel you up the success curve or down the failure curve.

> The individual who wants to reach the top in business must appreciate the might of the force of habit—and must understand that practices are what create habits. He must be quick to break those habits that can break him—and hasten to adopt those practices that will become the habits that can help him achieve the success he desires.
>
> — J. Paul Getty

It's interesting to note where your habits really come from. They arise out of your actions, true—but where do your actions come from? Remember this?

your philosophy *creates* your attitude your actions your results *creates* your life

Your habits come from your daily activities compounded over time. And your activities are the result of the choices you make in the moment. Your choices come from your habits of thought, which are the product of your thinking, which comes from the view you have of the world and your place in it—your philosophy.

Which is why the key to your success, to mastering the Slight Edge through the long-term effect of your everyday habits of thought and action, is your philosophy.

The point of this book is to give you a structure for designing your success. Once you are aware of and understand how to use the Slight Edge to work for you, you can go about succeeding on purpose. Your intuitive sense of the Slight Edge becomes your automatic pilot. It guides you, keeps you on track and helps you measure your progress. It weighs and measures your every habit, discarding those that don't serve you and designing new ones that do.

The key is making those right choices.

Each choice you make is like a length of steel wire. By itself, it's not that big a deal, but when braided together, when compounded with all the other choices you make, these lengths of wire form a thick cable of awesome strength and power.

> Nothing is stronger than habit.
>
> —Ovid

Have you ever seen the huge steel cables that hold up suspension bridges like the Golden Gate Bridge in San Francisco or the Verrazzano-Narrows Bridge in New York? They're flexible, yet they're so thick and strong you get the sense that no earthly force could break them. The cables made up of your right choices are just like those cables. So are the ones made from your wrong ones. The cables made from your right choices uphold and support you. Those made from wrong choices imprison and restrain you. These cables are your habits of thought and attitude.

Want to know where the Slight Edge is taking you? Look at your predominant habits of thought (my friend John Fogg calls them your "habitudes") and the kinds of choices you habitually make. It's these habits that are taking you up the success curve or down the failure curve of the Slight Edge.

Your habits operate at the unconscious level; you are not normally aware of them. It's only by bringing a habit into your conscious awareness that you can observe what it's doing, how it empowers and serves you or doesn't. By developing Slight Edge thinking (and especially by harnessing the next power we'll talk about, the power of reflection), you'll shine the bright light of awareness on your habits.

Once you're aware of a habit that doesn't serve you, how do you change it or get rid of it? It takes time—and it takes knowing where to focus your energy.

Trying to get rid of an unwanted habit is a bit like trying not to think about an elephant (the more you try not to think about it, the more you think about it). That's because what you focus on, grows. Which is why people who put a lot of energy into focusing on what they don't want, by talking about it, thinking about it, complaining about it or fretting about it, usually get precisely that unwanted thing.

It's tough to get rid of the habit you don't want by facing it head on. The way to accomplish it is to *replace* the unwanted habit with another habit that you do want. And creating new and better habits, ones that empower and serve you, is something you know how to do. You do it the same way you built any habit you have: one step at a time. Baby steps. The Slight Edge.

Harness the Power of Reflection

In my business, I often see people make the mistake of thinking they are being productive because they are being busy. Being productive and being busy are not necessarily the same thing. Doing things won't create your success; doing *the right things* will. And if you're doing the wrong things, doing more of them won't increase your odds of success—it will only make you fail faster!

Nobody sets out to fail. We all believe we're headed down the right path, or at least, a reasonably right one. People get out of bed, go to work and work hard. They love their families. They put smiles on their faces. They do everything they're supposed to do and they think they've had a progressive day, or at least set out to have one. And all too often, what really happened is that they spent the day treading water like a duck swimming upriver against a strong current, its little webbed feet flailing away underneath but getting him nowhere.

Everybody's busy. Everyone does the actions. But were they the right actions? Were those actions productive? Did you take a step forward?

These are questions that most people never take the time to think about.

Did you eat well, or did you eat badly? Who did you associate with today? Did they empower you? How? In what way? Did you listen to good information today, or just zone out to the music? Did you engage in positive conversation, or did you gossip or complain? What did you read that contributed to your success today? Did you do any of the things unsuccessful people aren't willing to do? Whose dream did you build today—yours or somebody else's?

In the 12-Step System, this is called "taking a searching and fearless personal inventory." I honestly encourage you to get a little searching and fearless with yourself. Keep your progress—or the lack of it—in your face!

Here's a powerful exercise: Instead of writing down what you're *going* to do (chances are you've been doing that your entire life anyway, and it doesn't make you any better at doing them!), write down at the end of the day what you *did* do that day. What actions did you take today that made you successful?

Did you read ten pages of a good book? Did you eat healthy food and get some good exercise? Did you engage in positive associations? Did you do the things you need to do to be successful in your business? Did you tell somebody, "I love you"?

At the end of a week, look back over your lists and take inventory. Not only will it tell you a lot about the truth of your everyday life, chances are good that the mere act of recording this daily reflection will have already started changing what you do!

Here's what this exercise did for me the first time I did it: After the first few days, I found that by 10:00 in the morning, I was changing my normal course for the day and engaging in more positive Slight Edge actions—because I didn't want to face that man in the mirror empty-handed again that night!

There are lots of different ways to practice consistently self-reflection, and I don't necessarily recommend one over another, simply because everyone's different and what works best for me may not work best for you.

Some people accomplish this by keeping a journal. If you choose this approach, here's the key to making it work: don't just write down a record of what happened today, along with your thoughts and feelings about what happened. Ask yourself the specific Slight Edge questions. *In each area of my life, what are the critical, simple little things that are easy to do, and easy not to do? Did I do them? Did I move forward? Did I ride on the success curve?*

Some like keeping a journal sporadically, but find it difficult to keep up day in and day out, and instead create a specific, written list of Slight Edge actions that they consult and check off every day. On days they don't make time to write an entry in their journal, they at least go through the list and ask themselves those questions: *In each area of my life, did I do those things that are easy to do, and easy not to do? Did I continue my momentum on the success curve?*

Some would rather talk than write, and prefer to keep track of the day's actions out loud, in conversation. You can find a Slight Edge buddy, a friend who also wants to harness the power of reflection, and schedule a little time together or on the phone to debrief each other. *How did the day go? In each area of my life, did I ... ?* Doing this every day is ideal, but you can still make it work very well with a twice-a-week call, or even a once-a-week call. The key is consistency; like the tortoise, steady wins the race.

More and more, people are choosing to achieve a higher level of productivity through reflection by working with a coach. Only ten or fifteen years ago, most people thought of "coaching" only in the context of athletics. Then people realized that they had way better chances of pursuing their fitness goals if they used a personal trainer.

Soon, high-level business executives started using individual consulting sessions with productivity consultants to "coach" them in their high-stakes financial and organizational game. And in the last few years, the dam burst: people suddenly realized they could hire a coach for anything and everything, and the field of "personal coaching" exploded as one of the hottest new occupations.

So, what does a coach do? More than anything else, a coach holds up a mirror and shows you what you're doing, day in and day out. A coach keeps the Slight Edge in your face. A coach helps you harness the power of reflection.

Whatever method you choose to use, find some way to make reflection an everyday thing, day in and day out, without fail.

When what you didn't improve one day is clear to you and you're aware of it, by 10:00 the next morning you'll be hunting for self-improvements like a heat-seeking missile. You'll be reading, listening, associating to and with things and people that empower you. You won't be able to help it! You'll become so motivated that nothing—*nothing*—will prevent you from improving.

Harness the Power of Celebration

There is another critical reason the power of reflection is so important. It's not just to be a nag and remind you when you're slacking off. It's also to point out to you all the positive steps you're taking.

Over twenty years ago, authors Ken Blanchard and Spencer Johnson wrote, "People who feel good about themselves produce good results." The little book in which these words appeared, *The One Minute Manager*, became one of the decade's most influential business books. Blanchard and Johnson coined what has become one of the most well worn phrases in business: they urged managers and business owners not to walk around trying to catch people doing something wrong, but to "catch them doing something right," and then acknowledge it on the spot. They called this a "one minute praising."

It's easy to forget to catch yourself doing something right.

If you have kids, chances are better than even that you can still remember the moment they took their first step. Chances are good that step got noticed and celebrated, big time. And chances are even better that within a week, they were walking around for hours a day and nobody even gave it a second thought—including them.

I heard a story once about a woman who had reached a point in her early fifties where she felt she was so badly starving for affection, she didn't know if she could continue in her marriage. She told her husband how she felt, and said that for years, she had been unable to tell if he still loved her or not.

Her husband was genuinely perplexed. "But I told you I love you thirty years ago," he exclaimed. "Why would you think anything changed?" Poor man: it had never occurred to him that it's not enough to say, "I love you" one time. It's something that needs saying every day, and not only in words, but in actions, too, especially those little, thoughtful things that say, "I'm thinking about you and I care about you."

It's the Slight Edge power of reflection and acknowledgement—celebration.

Keep your Slight Edge activities, your right choices and incremental successes, right out in the open where you can see them and celebrate them. Remember that all the activity ever required to apply the Slight Edge for your success is nothing but a series of baby steps. Trust the process. Acknowledge those steps, no matter how small or insignificant they may seem at the time.

Is it easy to do? Yes. Easy not to do? Yes. If you don't do it, will it destroy you? No ... but that simple error in judgment, compounded over time, will ruin your chances for success.

Make each successful right choice a celebration. You'll be able to feel, literally, those balance scales shifting in your favor. Nothing breeds success like more success.

CHAPTER 9

Mastering Yourself

> No stream rises higher than its source. Whatever man
> might build could never express or reflect more than
> he was. He could record neither more nor less than he
> had learned of life when the buildings were built ...
> His philosophy, true or false, is there.
>
> — Frank Lloyd Wright

The greatest gift you could ever give yourself is also the wisest business investment you could ever make. It is also the most critical step in accomplishing any challenging task, and is the one step without which all other success strategies, no matter how brilliant or time-tested, are doomed to fail.

What is this mysterious gift? It is *your own personal development*. Investing in your own improvement, your own personal growth and betterment, is all these things and more.

Abraham Lincoln said, "Give me six hours to chop down a tree, and I will spend the first four hours sharpening the axe." In other words, he would spend twice as much time working on himself as on the task itself.

What do most people do? They grab the axe, dull or not, and start whaling away at the tree. And if they aren't making a major dent in that tree pretty soon, they quit—and probably mutter something about how it's the tree's fault!

How you swing the axe, how hard, in what arc and with what rhythm on exactly what spot you hit the tree—all these are strategies that concern your actions, and they can all be measured, weighed, and improved ... but it starts with the axe itself. And the axe is you.

Results Come Last

It is easy to be seduced by the promise of results. We live in a results-oriented world, a culture that overwhelmingly measures the success of a course of action by its results. Talk is cheap, after all—and what is it that really matters? Results. The bottom line. Show me. Proof of the pudding's in the eating, right?

But there is a problem here. There's a flaw in this thinking. In fact, the flaw in this thinking is so profound; ninety-five percent of all people's efforts are ending up as failure! And what is so remarkable is that this isn't some deep, hidden, subtle flaw. It's so obvious, everyone ought to see it—but it's so deeply ingrained in our culture, nearly everyone is hypnotized into missing it.

Here is the flaw: How can you judge the course of action you're taking by its results, when its results come last?

The problem with focusing on results is simply that it doesn't work. Having your attention on your results is like driving your car by looking in the rearview mirror. Your results live in the past, and like all things in the past, they belong there.

What you can do with your results is learn from them. Results are valuable feedback. Let them help motivate and guide your tomorrows. But a focus on results only takes you out of the present moment where the action really is.

What about your actions?

Many approaches to personal and professional development I have observed go deeper than results by focusing instead on your actions as the place to bring about positive change. That's a logical place to start looking, but the problem is that your actions are not the source of your success or failure.

Again, that's why diets don't work; they can't. They're doomed to fail because most diets dictate what your actions should be. They don't deal with where your actions come from.

What about attitudes?

Again, most popular approaches to personal and professional development understand the power of attitude as well, and put some of their focus on taking you behind the actions to look at your attitudes.

But this approach is still not getting to the heart of the matter—and you already know why, because this is where we started out in Chapter 1 of this book:

The only reliable, consistent way to control your attitudes— that control your actions, which control your results—is to control your thoughts. And the source of your thoughts is your philosophy. This is why the master entrepreneur W. Clement Stone uttered these often-quoted words: "What the mind of man can conceive and believe, the mind of man can achieve."

Your philosophy is your paradigm, your view of the way life is. It is how you say life works or doesn't work, and determines everything about the course of actions you'll choose *and keep choosing over time.* Your philosophy is the foundation upon which you build your life. There is nothing more fundamental or essential.

Your philosophy is the source of your failure or success. It is the garden in which your beliefs grow—and your beliefs lay the fertile groundwork for everything else. The Slight Edge will either promote you or expose you for who and what you really are—and who and what you are comes from your philosophy.

In the Sermon on the Mount, Jesus spoke of two types of foundation. He spoke about the "wise man" who built his house upon the rock: "And the rain descended, and the floods came, and the winds blew, and burst against that house; and yet it did not fall, for it had been founded upon the rock."

And then he told of a second character—a "foolish man" who built his house on sand: "And the rain descended, and the floods came, and the winds blew, and burst against that house; and it fell and great was its fall."

The foundation upon which you are building the house of your life is what will determine the nature of the house itself. Will the house stand? Will it fall apart? Will it leak, or will it withstand whatever weather nature throws at it? What results will your life produce? It's a critically important question—because by the time the results are in, the outcome will already be pretty well determined. You can't wait for your results to judge your actions. You can't wait to see what kind of house you've got before you judge whether or not it had a sturdy foundation!

Your success will always be the *progressive realization* of a worthy ideal. Your philosophy comes first; your results come last. And this brings us to the most important Slight Edge strategy of all.

Continuous Learning

> The trouble with the world is not that people know too little,
> but that they know so many things that ain't so.
>
> — Mark Twain

We've talked about all sorts of forces you can harness to help power your path through life. The most important force of all, the force the drives the whole process of living with the Slight Edge, is the power of *continuous learning*.

When I say "learning," I don't mean simply learning from school, although schooling certainly has its place. And I don't just mean learning from books or from a teacher—though you already know that I revere the knowledge to be gained from good books, and I feel the same way about great teachers, too. I'm also not just talking here about learning from the example of others, from advice from your friends, from the "school of hard knocks," or learning from your mistakes ...

I don't mean any one of those ... I mean *all* of them! Once you've set foot on the path of mastery and grasped the philosophy of the Slight Edge, educating yourself through any and all means available is the critical process that will keep you on that path and make the Slight Edge work for you.

I also don't mean "education" in the more narrowly defined sense of learning specific skills or subjects. Naturally, you need to pursue continuous learning in order to acquire the knowledge and skills involved in mastering any subject or pursuit that will contribute to your personal and professional growth and development. But it's more than simply a matter of acquiring specific knowledge. Continuous, lifelong learning is the material from which you continually build your philosophy—and by now, you and I both know how important that is! Learning is also the material from which you build your awareness, and *that* is also critical in mastering the Slight Edge.

After getting out of high school, fifty-eight percent of all high school graduates who don't go on to college *never read a book again!* When I first read that figure, I was shocked ... but not surprised. That's one reason the ninety-five percent give up and slide down the failure curve. They spend their lives building someone else's dream, not because they aren't capable of building their own, but because they never gain the knowledge they need.

Illiteracy is a much greater problem today than many people realize. Of the slightly more than six billion people on earth, according to the Wycliffe organization, one billion cannot read! Can you imagine that?! One person out of every six—one *billion* people— cannot read, and that rate is on the rise.

But consider this: If you are one of that fifty-eight percent who never reads after high school, what's the difference between you and the billion people around the world who couldn't read if they wanted to? No difference at all.

Of course, simply reading won't necessarily put you on the success curve. Remember my shoeshine woman and her little pile of novels? No question about her literacy—the woman loved to read. But where would she have been if that pile had included Norman Vincent Peale, Dale Carnegie, Zig Ziglar, Jim Rohn, *The Millionaire Next Door, Smart Women Finish Rich,* and any of the hundreds and thousands of other inspirational, educational, empowering books out there? Where would she have been if for the previous year or two, she'd read just ten pages, one chapter, of those books in between customers?

You know where she'd be.

When was the last time you attended a seminar or took an adult-education class, not because you were required to, but simply to improve yourself? When was the last time you went bowling? If your bowling average is over 200, congratulations! You're a heck of a bowler—and you may want to rethink your priorities. If you lined up the one hundred most successful men and women in America and calculated their bowling averages, I bet they wouldn't break 70. The average American will go bowling 233 times in his or her life—and they all have something better to do. I know bowling is one of the most popular pastimes in the United States, but wouldn't you rather have success be your most popular pastime?

I'm not picking on bowling, or any other form of recreation. We need balance in our lives, and taking time at the bowling alley can also serve you in all sorts of ways—your fitness, your relationships with your friends, your ability to let work go, to relax and have fun. All good things ... but the question is, are you developing yourself? Are you building your dream or only your boss's?

Read just one chapter of an information-rich, inspiring book every day. Listen to fifteen minutes of a life-transforming audiocassette or CD. Take a course or seminar every few weeks or months.

Are these things easy to do? Sure. And those simple disciplines compounded over time, like a penny doubled every day for a month, will send you up to the top. Are they easy not to do? No question. And if you don't do them, will you destroy your life today? Of course not. But that simple error in judgment, compounded over time, will pull you down the curve of failure and take away everything you've hoped for and dreamed about ... forever!

"Book Smarts" vs. "Street Smarts"

> Q: Five frogs sat on a lily pad. One decided to jump off. How many were left?
>
> A: Five ... all of them are still sitting there. The one frog only *decided* to jump.

The famous Chinese proverb says, "The journey of a thousand miles starts with a single step"—another wonderful example of traditional Slight Edge wisdom. But note: The journey starts with a single step—not with *thinking* about taking a step!

Plenty of people accumulate knowledge but still dwell on the failure curve. It's not only the quantity of knowledge that sets and keeps your course, but also the quality of knowledge. There are different types of knowledge and different avenues of learning; if you want to stay grounded and move ahead at the same time, you need a balance.

There are three principle kinds of learning. The first is *learning by study*, which includes reading, listening to audiocassettes and CDs, and attending classes and seminars. The second type is *learning by doing*.

As passionate as I am about improving yourself by studying with great teachers, through great books, tapes, CDs and other media, I also know that all the study in the world won't build your business, establish your health, or create a happy, fulfilling family life. That takes your getting up and *doing it*. Book smarts is not enough: all true success is built from a foundation of study plus street smarts.

Life is not a spectator sport; there is no practice session. You've been immersed in it from day one; life lives in the right-here-right-now. That's why Emerson, who was an exceptionally well-educated man in the traditional book-smarts sense, advised, *Do the thing, and you shall have the power.*

Note that this is not a reversible philosophy. You can't just go get the power and *then* do the thing—though people do try to do it that way, and they spend their entire lives gathering the power ... and doing nothing.

Do the thing, and you shall have the power. The only way to have the power is to do the thing. Just do it. That's learning by doing.

In my marketing business, I'm often asked for the key to success. "What's the one thing I can do to guarantee my success?" My answer is always the same: "Be here, actively immersed in the process, one year from now." That's really the only right answer. It's the Slight Edge answer. You can't build your dream by what you're going to do or planning to do or intend to do. You only build your dream by building it.

If you aren't doing, you're dying. Life *is* doing.

The Rhythm of Learning

Knowledge without practice is useless.
Practice without knowledge is dangerous.

— Confucius

I can read a book like *As a Man Thinketh*, return it to my book-shelf, then come back a year later to read it again—and it feels like somebody sneaked into my room while I was sleeping and completely rewrote the book! Why? Because of the learning by doing I've gone through in the interim. My experiences have changed my perspective. Now, when I read a particular passage or point the author makes, I understand it in a way I could not have possibly seen a year ago. And that in turn informs my behavior: now, when I go to engage in my activity of the next day, I can apply what I've learned from James Allen in a way that I would not have thought of even twenty-four hours ago.

Book smarts, street smarts. Learning by study, learning by doing. Read about it, apply it, see it in action, take that practical experience back to my reading, deepen my understanding, take that deeper understanding back to my activity ... it's a never-ending cycle, each aspect of learning feeding the other. Like climbing a ladder: right foot, left foot, right foot, left foot.

Can you imagine trying to climb a ladder with only your right foot?

The two work together. What's more, they not only work better together, each amplifying the other, but the truth is, they really cannot work separately. At least not for long.

You can't go to the top based purely on knowledge learned in study; you can't go to the top purely through knowledge gleaned through action. The two have to work together. You study, and then you do activity. The activity changes your frame of reference, and now you are in a place where you can learn more. Then you learn more, and it gives you more insight into what you experienced in your activity, so now you re-approach activity with more insight. And back and forth, it goes.

This back-and-forth rhythm is worth noting. It is the rhythm of success.

Remember when we talked about "baby steps"? This learning-and-doing sense of rhythm is something you learned even before you learned to walk, and it's even more basic. Psychologists have found crawling is one of the most important activities we ever accomplish, because it profoundly affects the brain and its capacity to learn. The right-hand-left-leg, left-hand-right-leg rhythm of alternation acts upon our nervous systems like the surf upon the coastline, developing it, shaping it, and preparing it for all sorts of more sophisticated levels of learning and awareness later in life.

You've hear the expression, "Before you can walk, you have to crawl." There is more profound truth to this than most of us ever realized. That alternating rhythm, and your capacity to coordinate the behavior of opposites, is a critical Slight Edge skill. Balancing book smarts and street smarts is one aspect of that, and so is the daily success strategy that we'll look at next: course correction.

Course Correction

> You return again and again take the proper course—guided by what? By the picture in mind of the place you are headed for ...
> — John McDonald

What's the shortest path between two points? A straight line, right? Wrong. While that might be true in theory, it's never true in reality. And reality is where you and I live—and where we succeed or fail.

Have you driven on any roads lately that are perfectly straight? Even when you're on one of those interstates that seems like a long straight line to forever, do you hold the steering wheel perfectly still? Or do you move it back and forth, constantly correcting the direction the car is headed? That constant moving of the steering wheel is so familiar, it's second nature, and you probably never think about it. But if decided to hold the wheel rigidly in place, you'd be off the road, probably in less than a minute.

And in case you think that's just a matter of engineering, or of imperfections in the road's surface, this next example may come as a bit of a shock:

On its way to the moon, the miracle of modern engineering that is an Apollo rocket is actually on course only two or three percent of the time; for at least ninety-seven percent of the time it takes to get from the Earth to the moon, it's *off course*. In a journey of nearly a quarter of a million miles, the vehicle is on track for only 7,500 miles ... or to put it another way, for every half-hour the ship is in flight, it is on course for less than sixty seconds!

And it gets to the moon?! How is that possible?

Because modern space travel is a masterful example of the

Slight Edge in action.

If this machine, one of the most sophisticated, expensive and finely calibrated pieces of technology ever devised was correcting its own off-course errors twenty-nine minutes out of every thirty, is it reasonable to expect that you could do better than that? And even if you were able to match the rocket's degree of accuracy, you'd still be perfectly on target, on track and on course no more than ten days *per year!*

For anyone who lacks a grasp of the Slight Edge, being off course is something to be avoided at all costs. After all, if you're off course, you're failing, right? But those who understand the Slight Edge embrace Thomas Watson's philosophy about failure. Here is a more extended version of what he said:

> Would you like me to give you the formula for success? It's quite simple, really. Double your rate of failure ... You're thinking of failure as the enemy of success. But it isn't at all ... You can be discouraged by failure—or you can learn from it. So go ahead and make mistakes. Make all you can. Because, remember that's where you'll find success. On the other side of failure.
>
> — Thomas J. Watson, Sr.

Remember, the rocket got there. And so can you. Why? Because of continuous course correction.

What enabled the rocket to continue to make those adjustments that brought it back on track to reach its destination? The adjustments were all done by a computerized guidance system, the heart of which was a gyroscope.

A gyroscope is a spinning mass mounted in a base that retains the same orientation no matter in what direction the base itself is going. You may have played with a toy gyroscope as a child—the kind you wind up with a string like a top, make it spin, and no matter how you hold it or what you do to it, it remains upright as long as it's spinning around. The force created by that toy gyroscope is so powerful it can balance on the tip of your finger or dance upright along a string.

The rocket starts from point A (its current position) and heads for point B (the moon). As it travels its first few miles, it gets slightly off course. Now the rocket's gyroscope shows one reading, while the rocket's instruments show that it's actually headed in a slightly different direction. The gyroscope, remember, is always pointed in the *right* direction, the direction the ship actually wants to go.

The computer processor detects that the rocket's off course and tells it to make an adjustment. If the processor and the rocket were speaking English, the conversation might sound something like this:

Processor: "Rocket, you're 1.27 degrees north—bring it back to 1.29."

Rocket: "Okay ... done."

Processor: "Good ... Whoa, that's too much, now you're 1.30—move it 0.01 degrees south."

Rocket: "No problem, I'll do that, too."

Processor: "Great—no, wait, too far west. Adjust course 0.067 degrees."

Rocket: "Got it, consider it done."

Processor: "Whoops, too much, come back 0.012."

Rocket: "Right, 0.012 ... how's that?"

Processor: "Little too far north again, ease back to 1.27 ... "

And so it goes, from here to the moon, a constantly occurring series of adjustments turning what is predominantly a string of failures into ultimate success.

You have a gyroscope, too, and it works in much the same way, if you allow it to. Your gyroscope is your vision of where you're going—in other words, your dream. Your processor is the Slight Edge: a consistent series of tiny, seemingly insignificant actions, easy to do and easy not to do, and in this case, doing them leads you directly to the moon instead of shooting off into the vacuum of outer space.

You're hungry. There's a bunch of greasy junk food in a vending machine beckoning you. Your gyroscope is spinning—it's focused on your health. Your processor goes, *click ... click ... whirr* ... and you choose a salad or a piece of fruit instead.

There's a display rack of books and magazines. You reach towards the copy of People because it has a juicy piece of gossip you'd just love to read—about a movie star you can't stand but it looks really intriguing anyway—and it's only a few bucks and you've got some time over lunch, and—*Click ... whirr ... click ...* and instead you decide to go back to your car for your copy of *Smart Women Finish Rich*. Or to take a twenty-minute walk in the park.

You're having coffee with friends and they start bitching and complaining about their work, their bosses, their jobs ... *Click ... click ... whirrrrr ...* and you find a way to change the subject because you know that if the talk doesn't get onto a positive track within another sixty seconds, you'll find a reason to excuse yourself.

Click ... click ... whirr ...

Knowing the Slight Edge, you make the adjustment automatically. You make those right choices, the ones that serve you. You do those simple, seemingly insignificant things that forward your progress up the success curve. You read good books. You listen to motivating tapes. You hang around successful people who empower you. You're a five percenter, a winner, a success.

Once you know the Slight Edge, you know that in getting from point A to point B you'll be off track most of the time. And you know that it's the adjustments—those little, seemingly insignificant corrections in direction—that have the most power in your life.

Kaizen: **Plan, Do, Review**

You know this saying: "Ready ... aim ... " and what comes next? "Fire!" right? That's the way it's usually put—but there's a better way.

Ready, fire, aim!

The problem with "Ready, aim, fire" is that in the real world, where everything is in motion and things are constantly changing, by the time you've finished all that readying and aiming, the target is long gone!

Here's another way of saying *ready, fire, aim*: plan, do, review.

"Plan, do, review" is an approach to learning that began gaining credibility in educational institutions toward the end of the twentieth century, and it's used in some of the better schools today. It's a Slight Edge strategy.

Students *plan* what they're going to learn and create their own activities and experiments for study. Then, they *do* what they planned. And then they *review* their planning and doing to see if anything was missing to help them learn what could be done to improve the process and the results they've accomplished. Then they plug those new insights into their next plan, and they're off and running up the Slight Edge curve to success.

The operative Slight Edge strategy at work here is the constant and consistent back-and-forth of doing actions and correcting those actions—course correction, just like the moon rocket. What this strategy produces is what business management philosophy has come to call "continuous improvement," a concept that the Japanese call *kaizen*.

This idea was introduced to Japan after World War II by an American, W. Edwards Deming. A remarkable statistician, Dr. Deming consulted and lectured Japanese industrial leaders about "total quality." He taught that "the system is the solution"—and showed how it's always the source of the problem as well.

Remember what happened to the Japanese and American auto industries in the '70s and '80s? The Japanese ate America's lunch in the marketplace. Know why? Slight Edge strategy. They had it; we didn't.

The Japanese took Deming's Slight Edge teachings about simple little disciplines in improving quality, compounded them over time, and in less than a decade they blew the much larger, richer and more powerful industry leader (the United States) out of the water. So far out of the water, in fact, that the top-selling car in America for years was the Honda.

It wasn't that the Americans didn't improve. The 1983 Chevy was clearly superior to the 1973 Chevy. But General Motors kept looking for those big breakthroughs, while the Japanese kept making little, seemingly insignificant improvements which, compounded over time, enabled them to steal the spotlight in what was once almost exclusively an American car show. The Japanese had major automotive breakthroughs, too, but they were the result of their Slight Edge strategy.

In the 1990s, the American auto industry made quite a comeback: great cars, record sales and profits. It was a stunning turnaround, and what turned it around were our automakers finally embracing the teachings of W. Edwards Deming: that a commitment to developing and sticking to a Slight Edge strategy will absolutely, positively send you to the top.

Plan, do, review (and *ready, fire, aim!*) creates a structure and support system for continuously improving. It's the strategy of constant course correction. You may have heard the expression, "It's not how you plan your work, it's how you work your plan." Not quite. A Slight Edge strategy means doing both at once—one tiny, course-correcting step at a time.

The Slight Edge is the process. You choose which way it goes: up with the five percent, or down with the other ninety-five percent. You don't just make that choice once and then say, "Ahh, I'm finished, now I'm all set." You make that choice moment to moment to moment—and keep making it, every month and every day, for the rest of your life.

Each new moment will present you with a new Slight Edge choice to be made. Before long it will become natural and automatic, but when you first begin, it will require your constant awareness.

You have to choose to make the Slight Edge work *for* you—moment by moment, one step at a time. Remember the rocket to the moon.

Is it easy to do? Yes. Is it easy not to do? Of course. If you don't do it, will your life collapse? No—not today. But that simple error in judgment, compounded over time, will pull you down the failure curve, absolutely and irrevocably, no questions asked. Unless you accept the wealthy man's third gift—the choice—and keep on accepting it, day by day and moment by moment.

Learning Through Modeling

Earlier I mentioned that there are three principal types of learning. We've examined the first two (learning through study and learning through doing) and you're probably wondering if we were ever going to get around to the third! In a way, I've saved the best for last, because utilizing this third type of learning will tremendously accelerate the first two.

It is *knowledge through modeling*.

Throughout human history (and long before there were such things as books, universities or continuing education programs) there has been one tried-and-true path for learning a skill, craft, art, trade or profession: go study with a master. All the great traditions of learning say the same thing: if you want to learn how to do something well, go find a master of that skill and apprentice yourself.

Like the "coaching" model, the "mentor/apprentice" model is experiencing a tremendous surge in popularity right now. Mentoring networks, agencies and organizations are springing up in all sorts of professions—and this doesn't surprise me in the least.

With the advent of the Internet culture, there's been an explosion in information over the past decade. Now we're starting to realize that information alone is not enough—and information plus personal experience (the "school of hard knocks") is not enough. We need some way to process all that information and experience and integrate it. And there is only one reliable, solid way to do that: find someone else who's already mastered an area, and model yourself on that person's experience.

To apply this principle doesn't require a formal mentor/apprentice relationship. Whatever goals you aspire to, just seek out people who have achieved the same or very similar goals, or who are well along that path, and go camp on their doorsteps or do whatever you can to associate with them, emulate them, let their grasp, understanding and mastery of the subject rub off on you.

If you want to raise the quality of your life, hang out with people who have been there and done that. If you want to be a great public speaker, spend time with great speakers. If you want to be a success in business, then find a way to spend time in the company of successful businesspeople. If it's important to you to be a terrific parent, the best thing you can do to further that aim is to spend lots of time with men and women who have mastered parenting.

You can define a society by the heroes it keeps. You can also define a person by the heroes he or she keeps. Who are your heroes? Who are you modeling yourself after?

The ninety-five percent on the failure curve tend to accept the heroes society plants in front of them: film stars (America's version of royalty), rock stars, sports stars. I can certainly admire these folks, but I always ask myself, *Can I emulate them?* Practically speaking, can I convert my admiration into constructive modeling that increases my learning and moves my own life forward?

Too often, we make heroes out of people who can't help us, whose lives are fantasies, not genuine role models. Take a look at who your heroes are—write down a list and examine it. Ask yourself, "Can I become like them? Are these people doing the kinds of things that I aspire to do and living the kinds of lives that I aspire live? Can they really help me become who I want to become?"

Find people who've done what you want to do and surround yourself with them. That's learning through modeling, and it's a powerful part of learning how to understand and use the Slight Edge.

The Law of Association

Do you remember a comment I made about income, way back in the very beginning of this book? While I was sitting in the Phoenix airport thinking about my new friend, the shoeshine woman, I mused over this thought:

Your income tends to equal the average of the incomes of your five best friends.

This principle does not apply solely to your finances: it operates in every aspect of your life.

Your level of health will tend to be about the average level of health of your five best friends. Your personal development will be at about the average level of personal development of your five best friends. Your relationships, financial health, attitudes, level of success in your career, and everything else about your life will tend to be very close to the average level of each of these conditions in your five closest friends and associates.

We all understand this principle instinctively; our language is shot through with idioms that reflect it:

You're known by the company you keep.
Show me where you fish and I'll show you what you catch.
Birds of a feather flock together.

You are the combined average of the five people you associate with most—including the way you walk, talk, act, think and dress. Your income, your accomplishments, even your values and philosophy will reflect them.

If the five people around you have negative philosophies, it's virtually impossible for you to have a positive philosophy. If the five people around you are consistently complaining, living in the past, blaming others for their difficulties, and thinking and acting in a generally negative way, then what are the odds of you finding your way onto the success curve? Slim to none.

If you consistently associate with negative people, it's highly unlikely you will succeed at having and maintaining a positive approach to your life.

Become acutely aware of who you are modeling. This has everything to do with your philosophy and your attitudes, which has more to do with your actions and with what you're actually doing and creating in your everyday life, than any other factor.

The reason "birds of a feather flock together" is simply that they're all going in the same direction, headed for the same destination. Look at the people with whom you flock, the *company you keep*: what destination are they headed for? And is that where you want to be headed?

Look at the people around you. Are they more successful than you are? Are they people who live the kinds of lives you aspire to live, or the kinds of lives you hope to leave behind? On what side of the Slight Edge are they living—on the success curve or the failure curve? Is the Slight Edge working for them or against them? Where will they be in twenty years? And are they pulling you up or dragging you down?

This is a pass or fail test: there is no "maybe" about it. Remember, there is no standing still: we're all going in one of two directions, either up or down. Your association with each person you know is either empowering you, or it's not—taking you up the success curve or down the failure curve.

How can you tell? One way is to go back to the business of future and past, responsibility and blame. When you and this particular friend get together, are your conversations about responsibility, aspirations and taking initiative? Or do they often seem to work their way around to blame or its cousins—envy, jealousy, resentment and irritation?

Do your conversations focus more on the future or on the past? It's only natural, when you share a common history and set of experiences, to enjoy reminiscing over fond memories; that's not what I mean. What I mean is, does your relationship have a forward-looking, positive feeling to it, or do the two of you get together and always seem to end up circling events of the past, like a cat endlessly turning round and round before it can settle down to sleep?

If your relationship with someone has a theme of blame and feeds on the past, it's disempowering. If it has a theme of responsibility, self-reflection and change and feels like something moving into the future, it's empowering.

We are all either building our own dreams or building somebody else's. To put a finer point on it, we're either building our dreams—or building our nightmares.

There may be some people with whom you're now spending two days a week, where you might decide you need to take that down to two hours. There may also be people with whom you're spending only two minutes, where you'll realize you need to spend far more time with them—two hours or two days. And you will find times when what you really need to do is simply disassociate yourself from someone; that's a part of the Law of Association, too.

For many people, I think this can be a tough aspect of the Slight Edge to understand and accept. Most everything else about the Slight Edge, as you already know, is easy to do—but disassociating yourself from people who do not empower you can be a sad and difficult thing to do. Especially if you love them. Especially if they are old friends or dear family.

So take heart: by "disassociating," I don't necessarily mean cutting them out of your life completely. But casual relationships deserve casual time—not quality time. There are people with whom you can spend two minutes, but not two hours. There are people with whom you can spend two hours, but not two days.

This part of Slight Edge thinking requires a compassionate *awareness*. Having compassion and having direction are not mutually exclusive: they just take careful thought and discernment. You're not judging those people; you're simply asking yourself to be honest about whether or not those relationships are empowering you and helping to support your purpose and realize your dreams.

Leadership

I'm often asked, "How do I become a leader?" In our push-button, instant-everything world, people often seem to want to take an express route from the first stages of learning straight to leadership. But of course, it doesn't work that way.

How does it work? Leadership is not something you "do"; it is something that grows organically out of the natural rhythm of learning.

When you start at the beginning of anything, you're at the highest level of anxiety. As you learn—through study and doing, information and experience, book smarts and street smarts—you gradually lower your level of anxiety by raising your level of mastery.

As you continue climbing that ladder of knowledge (remember, right foot–left foot, right foot–left foot, study–action, study–action) you keep your eyes on worthy mentors, always using learning through modeling as your learning gyroscope to keep you on track.

Using those three dimensions of learning—study, do, model—with Slight Edge persistence, in time your level of mastery rises to the point where you turn around and realize others are modeling you! You have become worthy of emulating. The cream has become butter; the hyacinth of knowledge has covered the pond of your effort. You have grown into leadership.

How do you become a leader? Through honestly pursuing the path of self-mastery and continuous learning.

Your Mastermind

Of all the books I have ever encountered in my pursuit of excellence and of the philosophy as well as the how-to's of success, Napoleon Hill's masterpiece *Think and Grow Rich* is the most influential. When you ask successful people what factors most contributed to their success, this is the book they will most commonly cite.

During the twenty years it took Napoleon Hill to write *Think and Grow Rich*, he interviewed more than five hundred of the richest and most successful men and women in the world, and then painstakingly analyzed what he'd learned and spelled it out in the form of thirteen "success secrets." One of the most fascinating success secrets he learned that these people shared in common was what he termed the "Mastermind."

"No two minds ever come together without thereby creating a third, invisible, intangible force, which may be likened to a third mind," wrote Hill. A group of like-minded, achievement-oriented individuals, he explained, could come together to create an association far greater than the sum of its parts, thus dramatically leveraging each other's success.

As two examples from startlingly different sides of the spectrum of human endeavor, he cites Henry Ford and Mahatma Gandhi as masters of the Mastermind principle, which he defines as: "The coordination of knowledge and effort of two or more people, who work toward a definite purpose, in the spirit of harmony."

Applying Hill's principle is simple: surround yourself with people of like mind and different talents and temperaments with the purpose of serving the goals of every member of the group. Associate with these people on a regular basis.

Remember that you're always dealing with gravity: one against nineteen, all the time. The ninety-five percent will always tend to be cynical, skeptical and negative; even when motivated by the best of intentions, they will attack you and bring you down.

Apply the Law of Association. Create your own Mastermind, a group of those who have chosen to live among the five percent, and let them support you, let them be the lift beneath the wings of your dreams.

CHAPTER 10

Turning Your Dreams into Reality

Whatever you can do, or dream you can, begin it.
Boldness has genius, power and magic in it.
— Johann Wolfgang von Goethe, *Faust*

There are entire books written about how to set, pursue and achieve your goals, and some of them are actually pretty good. You may or may not need an entire book; that's up to you. I like to keep things as *simple* as possible, because simple is usually far more effective—and most importantly, *simple* is what works best with the Slight Edge. Remember "easy to do," and you won't stray far from having your hands on the Slight Edge.

While everyone has a somewhat different approach to goal setting, there are four simple and fundamental steps you need to take for your dreams to turn into reality. Everyone who has ever created success, whether consciously or not, whether using this specific language or not, has gone through these four steps. They are the four universal truths of reaching for a big dream.

For a goal to come true:
You must write it down, make it specific and give it a deadline;
You must look at it every day;
You must understand and pay the price;
You must have a plan to start with.

Step One: Write It Down

The most critical skill of achieving success in any area whatsoever, from sports to high finance, radiant health to fulfilling relationships, is the skill of *envisioning*. Envisioning something simply means having the ability to create a vivid picture of something that hasn't factually happened yet, and make that picture so vivid that it feels real.

Envisioning doesn't happen simply by creating a picture in your mind. If your dreams and aspirations are happening in your mind only, that's not envisioning, that's wishful thinking. It's like saying, "I'll give it a try"—which as Yoda pointed out, really doesn't cut it. ("Do or do not—there is no *try*.")

Envisioning means quite literally making something up out of thin air—and *making it real*. By definition, you can't do that within the confines of your skull. It needs to become physical; it needs to involve your senses. In other words, you need to write it down. Making pictures of it, which people sometimes call a "dream board," is even better. Speaking it out loud is most powerful of all. But at the very least, write it down. The moment you do, it has started to become real.

What do you dream about? Pick a dream you have, any dream: your dream house, your dream car, dream vacation, dream job, dream marriage, dream career. Pick a dream that you'd really love to have come true. Write it on the first line below. Then pick another, and another, until you have five dreams.

If you're hesitating, know this: these dreams may be as huge or as small as you like; neither is "better" or more or less worthy to make real.

1. _____

2. _____

3. _____

4. _____

5. _____

Good. Now, let's have you add two descriptors that will make your dream more concrete: *what* and *when*.

First, go back to each dream and add whatever wording you need to make each dream absolutely specific. For example, if you had a dream to "be financially free," what does that mean, specifically? How much money do you need in the bank or investments, or coming in as annual income, to achieve what you call "financial freedom"? If there are any other conditions that need to be met (such as "being completely debt-free"), add those in, too.

What if one of your dreams is "radiant health." How would you make that specific? One way would be to describe exactly how you feel, what kinds of activities you engage in and what they feel like. Imagine reading your dream to someone you care about, and that person saying, "I'm not sure I quite grasp what you mean. Can you tell me exactly what you're shooting for?"

Now, the second descriptor: *when*? It's often been said, "Goals are dreams with deadlines." Let's reshape your dreams into goals by giving them deadlines. Go back through each dream and answer the question, "By when?"

You've probably heard of the Pareto Principle, known more popularly as "the 80/20 rule," which says that, for instance, twenty percent of the people in a sales force produce eighty percent of the results. (Vilfredo Pareto, an Italian economist who promulgated his theories around the turn of the twentieth century, actually arrived at his formula, which is a bit more complex than a simple 80/20 rule, to describe the tendency of wealth, innovation and initiative to concentrate in a self-selected elite, no matter what the external social or economic system. In other words, Pareto was really describing the success curve and failure curve—the two sides of the Slight Edge!)

Here is another application of Pareto's Law: eighty percent of everything you do tends to get done in the last twenty percent of the time available! If you don't create a concrete deadline, that last twenty percent never seems to arrive ... and you're always living in the eighty-percent time that says, "some day ... "

Write your dreams down; make them vivid and specific; give them a concrete timeline for realization; and you've taken a giant step towards making them real!

Step Two: Look at It Every Day

The single most compelling reason for writing down your dreams is so you can look at them and read them every day. The reason you need to look at them every day is the same reason you need to keep yourself in the company of positive people: you need to counteract the force of gravity—or to put a different name to it, the force of mediocrity.

Remember, it's nineteen to one—and you need to remind constantly your brain where it is you're headed or you'll drift away. If you don't keep yourself constantly, repeatedly focused on your destination, you'll be like a rocket ship without a gyroscope: you'll simply drift off gradually into the outer space of failure, never even coming remotely close to reaching the moon.

Surround yourself with it, keep your awareness in your face, look at it every single day. Your brain is far more complex and powerful than the biggest computer in the world, and your own subconscious is by far the biggest distraction you have.

Remember how many times you heard the word "No" by the time you hit first grade? Over 40,000 times—while you'd heard the word "Yes" only 5,000 times. Your brain has recorded an eight-to-one preponderance of "No," which translates into, "You can't do it ... It will never work ... That's impossible ... Why even bother trying?" We all come at this business of success with an extraordinary baggage of negative conditioning.

And that's all right. You and I can't live our childhoods over again, but we don't need to in order to fulfill our dreams. What we can do—and do need to do—is *surround ourselves with our own Yes's*. Surround yourself with messages that tell you your dreams are real, your dreams are real, your dreams are real.

Having your dreams concretely spelled out, on paper, in the most vivid and specific terms possible, and with a very tangible, concrete timeline, provides you with an "environment of Yes!" for your goals, dreams and aspirations. And when that nineteen-to-one force of gravity starts leaking from our subconscious and says, "Yeah, but are they really?"—we need to respond, *Yes! Yes! Yes! Yes! Yes!*

Here is the amazing thing—and I've seen this happen so many times, yet it never ceases to fill me with awe: when you set your goals, life has a way of rearranging itself, a series of events starts in motion that you could never have predicted or planned, to get you there. If you just sit there and try to figure it out, it doesn't happen. But when you surround yourself with your goals, your subconscious brain goes to work on it—and if you have the right philosophy, the philosophy of the Slight Edge, then you will come up with the right actions and keep repeating those actions ... and a series of events will kick in, including circumstances you could never have dreamed of, that will take you to that goal.

Step Three: Know and Pay the Price

Aha, there's the catch! I knew it! Here comes the big sacrifice ... so, what will I have to do? Throw away my television? Say goodbye to all fun and forego all my favorite foods? Give up a kidney?

Chances are, it's not quite that dramatic. Like anything else, when it comes to goals, we tend to see things like they're on the big screen; but they're not. Though your dreams may be big (in fact, I hope they're huge!), remember that the steps you're taking to get there are ... what, huge? No: small. Tiny. Baby steps. Easy to do.

The price you pay works the same way. You don't have to pay for your million-dollar dream with a million-dollar personal check. You can pay for it ... well, with a penny a day. But you do need to understand what that penny is, and you do need to pay it. Whatever the dream, whatever the goal, there's a price you'll need to pay, and that means something you'll need to give up.

It may be something as simple as giving up a type of junk food you're attached to, for the sake of your health; or something as subtle as giving up your right to be right, or your habit of exerting control over conversation for the sake of a relationship. It may mean postponing certain purchases or acquisitions, often called "delayed gratification," or letting go of some pleasures for the sake of the pursuit of a longer-term aim.

At a certain point in my life, when I'd suffered some huge setbacks and lost everything I had, I came to a critical point of decision. I'd been an athlete all my life, and at this point I'd become part of a softball team. We were serious, and we got pretty good. Before long, we were traveling and winning tournaments all over the place.

Then, I hit a point where I knew I had to get my career back on track. It was time to pick up the pieces, regroup and move on. I also knew I couldn't do this without changing something: I had to pay a price. It was a difficult choice, but I walked away from our softball team. My friends couldn't believe it. "You're quitting?!" And I said, "Hey you guys, you're still my friends, I love you, but get another outfielder." They're all still on that team today, still winning tournaments—and I took that same time and invested it elsewhere.

I had to plant and cultivate in a different field.

Remember, there aren't many millionaires who bowl over 100. Why not? Because they left the bowling league behind to build their fortunes. "Is that too large a price to pay?" is a question only you can answer. Remember this: whatever price you pay, there's a bigger price to pay for not doing it than the price for doing it. The price of neglect is much worse than the price of the discipline. It may take a few years to put your success on track—but it takes your entire life to fail.

Step Four: Start with a Plan

This is the point where people are often thrown off track. It's easy to assume that you need to put together the plan that will get you there—in other words, the *right* plan. The plan that will work. No. The point is not to come up with the brilliant blueprint that will take you all the way to the finish line. The point is simply to come up with a plan that will get you *out of the starting gate.*

You have to start with a plan, but the plan you start with will not be the plan that gets you there. Just for emphasis, I'm going to say that once more:

You have to start with a plan, but the plan you start with will not be the plan that gets you there.

What? That makes no sense at all! If this plan isn't going to get me to my goal, why bother designing it? What's the point? Aren't I just fooling myself with a pointless plan?

Not at all. You need a plan to start with, the same way you need a penny to start with before anything can double. The way you took your first baby step. The way you furrowed your brows, pursed your lips and struggled to sound out the first sentence you read.

Would that penny have financed an empire? Of course not.

Would that first step have won the Boston Marathon? Would that first sentence have earned you a Master's degree in literature? No, and no, and no. But without that penny, without that first wobbling step, without that first stumbling sentence, your dream—no matter how deeply you wanted it—would never have materialized.

People make the mistake of thinking they need the perfect plan. There is no perfect plan. By definition, there can't be, because *a plan is not getting there—it's only your jumping-off point.*

And that's the reason you need a plan: if you have no plan, there will be no jumping off. In fact, if you put too much energy into the plan, and make it too perfect, you're more likely to squelch all the life, spontaneity, intuition and joy out of the doing of it.

Do the thing, and you shall have the power. Don't try to figure it out! If you want twice the success, double your rate of failure.

You start with a plan, then go through the process of continuous learning through both study and doing, adjusting all the time through the *kaizen* of plan, do, review and then adjust—like a rocket to the moon, off track ninety-seven percent of the time, your gyroscope feeding information to your dream computer to bring you back on track ... You need a first plan so you can get to your second plan, so you can get to your third plan, so you can get to your fourth plan.

Success is the progressive realization of a worthy ideal. Keep holding that as your philosophy, and you will generate the attitudes and actions you need to keep progressively realizing a better and better plan.

Your starting plan is not the plan that will ultimately get you there ... but you need it so you have a place to start.

In my profession, training is a huge part of what drives the business. Training is the great equalizer: because we work with such large numbers and such a sweeping diversity of people from all types of backgrounds and walks of life, we train, train and train some more.

It's not that there's all that much to learn. It's like learning to play the piano: there are only twelve notes, after all. But to learn it, you need to hear it, and play it, over and over. It's as vivid an illustration of Slight Edge success as I've ever seen.

At the same time, I have very little regard for trainings that tell you, "This is exactly how you have to do it," because the actual sequence of actions and events that works will be different for everyone, every time. You can train people in the concepts, in how to think and what kinds of actions have worked, but you can't blueprint the specific sequence, because circumstances are always different.

This is why you need to have a plan to start with—but you cannot start with the plan that will get you there. You have to start with the philosophy that will take you; with the right *philosophy*, you'll find the plan.

To give you an example, here is the true story of how I built our company's largest sales and distribution organization in all of Germany, which has since become one of the largest such organizations in all of Europe and one of the most successful in the history of our industry.

Anatomy of a Breakthrough: How I Grew My German Organization

One Friday morning, I woke up and turned on the TV while I was getting dressed. On television, someone was talking about a business opportunity and franchise show in Albuquerque. I thought, *Hey, maybe I should be in that.* I called the people running the show, asked if they had an opening, they said, "Yeah," so I changed my plans for the day and spent the next eight or ten hours shopping around, buying things for my booth, and making little signs and packages to hand out.

The next morning I showed up at the franchise show and found my way to my little booth. I'd never done this before. I was surrounded by really nice, professional booths—and I stood in my stupid little homemade booth, trying to hand out my little brochures. Across from me, another person with a booth was blowing up balloons shaped like bears. There we were ... Bear Man and me.

All day long, people would come over to see the Bear Man's balloons and I would try to hand out my information, but nobody paid any attention to me. I had three hundred packages to give out and hoped to get names and phone numbers from maybe ten or twenty people—but I could not give my stuff away.

Finally, I found a line that worked. As one person walked past me to go see the Bear Man's balloons, I caught his eye and said, "Would you be interested in some great propaganda?" He stopped and laughed, and said, "Sure." I used that line for the entire weekend, gave out all three hundred packages and got about twenty names.

One of them happened to be a doctor named Shapiro. The next week, I called Dr. Shapiro; we had a pleasant conversation, but nothing happened as a result. I called him again, and kept calling him. After about a month and a half of following up with him, he came to meet with me, liked what he saw, and got involved with me in my business.

About this same time, I learned that our company was planning to open in Germany in about six months. I got my Mastermind group together and said, "Guys, this is it, we're going to open up Germany." They said, "How?" I had no idea how. The only thing I knew how to do was *double my rate of failure ... Do the thing and have the power*. We thought about it, and I decided what we needed to do was find Germans.

So at our meetings, we began teaching this amazing, sophisticated strategy we had developed: *Find Germans*.

Eventually somebody came up with the idea of dropping in on the local Mercedes dealership; someone else visited the local German club. One by one, ideas started to percolate.

About two weeks later, Dr. Shapiro showed up at a meeting and said, "Hey, I found a German." I asked him, "What do you mean?" He said, "I'm talking to my neighbor while he's mowing his lawn and I say, 'Hey by the way, Bob, do you know any Germans?' and he says, 'Well, yeah, I know a guy who lives in Germany,' and I say, *'Really?!'* "

I told Dr. Shapiro to send this German person all my information because I was planning to go over there in a few months. He said, "Hey, Jeff, aren't you giving a meeting over in Miami in a few months?" Yes, I was. "Well, this guy's coming over to the US and I think he's going to be in Miami then, too!"

A few months later, I go to Miami for my meeting there and sure enough, this fellow comes up to me afterwards and talks to me: his name is Vin, he's from Germany, and he gets quite excited about going back to Germany and being on the ground floor when we open up there in a few months ...

Except after Vin flies back to Germany, three months go by—and the company doesn't open in Germany after all. They have to delay the opening by at least another three or four months.

So I call Vin and tell him, "Hey, we're open in England, why don't you go over to England and start working over there? You can get a little English organization going as practice, and then when Germany does open up, you'll already know the ropes and be really ready."

So Vin and his wife Birgitte go to England, rent a little flat and start holding meetings there.

Now, one day Vin and Birgitte are walking to one of their meetings when they happen to stop to talk to a man who's painting a house. As they get talking, they ask him, "Hey, do you know anybody in Germany?" and he says, "Oh, yeah, I know this guy in Germany, he's really successful there."

Months later, when I finally get to Germany, I go from city to city, meeting with people in hotel lobby after hotel lobby—Hamburg, Düsseldorf, Cologne, Heidelberg, Munich, Frankfurt ... I don't know a thing about Germany, and I don't speak a word of German. But Vin and the housepainter's friend go with me, side by side, the whole time translating and helping me out, showing me around. At first, I'll be speaking to a group, then Vin will translate, then I'll say something else, then he'll translate. But soon something odd starts happening: I'll say something—and then he takes off in rapid-fire German and talk for five minutes straight before coming up for air. He doesn't need me to say anything else; he's doing fine without me!

By the time I left Frankfurt, the organization was launched—and today those two men are both multimillionaires, with the largest organization in all of Europe.

Now, here's the question I want to ask you: how did I plan that?! Maybe it was like this:

One day, I was sitting on my bed, putting on my socks, and

mumbling to myself, *Now how can I build a huge European organization?* I thought about that for a while, then slapped my forehead and said, "I got it! All I need to do is turn on the TV, they'll probably be talking about a franchise show—

"And if I go to the franchise show, chances are really good that I'll be stuck in a corner with some guy called the Bear Man who'll take everyone's attention off me so I won't have any success handing out my little brochures, which will make me figure out that what I should say to people is something like, 'Hey, would you be interested in some propaganda?' and if I do that not only will I hand out all three hundred of my little packages but I'll also get about twenty names—

"And one of those names will be a doctor from Albuquerque who won't really be that interested at first, but even though it could take me, oh, about three weeks of calling him, maybe the doctor will finally show up at one of my meetings where I'm training people about how to ask everyone if they know any Germans, and this doctor will get involved in my business and ask his next-door neighbor one day while he's cutting his grass (and it's a good thing it won't be raining that day, because then this carefully laid plan won't work) if he happens to know any Germans—

"And he will! He'll know this one person who not only lives in Germany, but happens to be coming over to Miami at the same time I'm going over there to give a meeting, which will work really well—

"Because even though he'll go back to Germany all excited about opening up there, if this plan works just right then that won't happen because it'll turn out that the company isn't ready to open up in Germany yet after all and that'll be just perfect because then I'll tell this guy, 'Hey, why don't you go over to England instead for a few months?' which my guess is he'll probably go ahead and do, maybe even renting a flat with his wife there and getting a little organization going—

"Which will be just perfect, just like I planned it, because one day when they're walking to one of their meetings they'll walk right past this house, which will be timed just right (because as luck would have it, it won't be raining on that day either!) so they'll stop and strike up a conversation with this housepainter, which is *perfect* because I will have trained them to ask, 'Hey, do you know any Germans?' so they'll ask that question and if this all goes just according to my plan then the housepainter won't even have to stop and think about it 'cause he'll just say, 'Yes, actually, I do know a fellow in Germany, and in fact he's quite a successful bloke over there,' and that'll be perfect too because when I do finally get over there and start holding meetings in Hamburg, even though it will look like I don't have the slightest clue about how I'm going to try and build an organization in Germany, the truth is that this guy who met me in Miami (the franchise show doctor's next-door-neighbor's friend) and the successful guy in Germany (the guy the Miami guy's neighborhood housepainter knows) will meet me in the hotel and travel with me as my trans-lators and because they'll be translating for me they'll understand the business better than anyone else I talk with by the end of visit—

"And then maybe those two guys will go on to build the largest sales and marketing organization in Germany, and one of the largest in all of Europe in the history of the business—

"Yeah ... " and I nodded sagely. "That should work ... Good plan, Olson!"

And I finished putting on my socks and shoes.

Do you think that's how it happened? Of course not! Then how did it?

The truth is, I *started with a plan*. My plan was this: I told peo-ple to ask their friends, "Do you know any Germans?" That was it. That was the plan.

And you know, it worked. A simple plan—you could even say, it was so simple it looked stupid. But if you start with a plan, and you practice those simple daily disciplines ... one plan leads to the next plan, leads to the next plan—

And soon you have one of the largest organizations in the his-tory of the industry.

Can you imagine how many times this ridiculously unlikely chain of events could have fallen apart? (Twice, an innocuous afternoon rain shower would have scuttled it!) Why didn't it? Because we started with a plan, and then allowed the Slight Edge to work.

Until one is committed there is always hesitancy, the chance to draw back, always ineffectiveness. Concerning all acts of initiative (and creation), there is one elementary truth, the ignorance of which kills countless ideas and splended plans; that the moment one definitely commits oneself, then Providence moves too. All sorts of things occur to help one that would never otherwise have occurred. A whole stream of events issues from the decision, raising in one's favor all manner of unforeseen incidents and meetings and material assistance, which no man could have dreamt would have come his way.

I have learned a great respect for one of Goethe's couplets:

"Whatever you can do, or dream you can, begin it.

Boldness has genius, power and magic in it."

— W. H. Murray
The Second Himalayan Expedition

A whole stream of events ... which no man could have dreamt would have come his way. That strikes me as a very good description of how our German organization came into being.

Don't try to figure out the whole race. Just figure out where to put your foot for the starting line. Just start. The result looks incredibly complex, but it's not; it never is. It's always the simple little things that take you there.

Everything you do, every decision you make, is either building your dream or building someone else's dream. Every single thing you do is either leading you away *from* the masses—or leading you away *with* the masses! Every single thing you do is a Slight Edge decision.

Our strategy for opening up in Germany seemed so ridiculously simple. What made the difference was that we did it every day. Did we have a German group after one day, one week, even one month? Of course not. We had nothing ... just a few names. And suddenly one day, those few names had blanketed Europe with a financial empire.

Just like the water hyacinth.

CHAPTER 11

Living the Slight Edge

Gentlemen, this is a football.

— Vince Lombardi

With these words, the legendary football coach would begin each new season of training, never taking anything for granted and always viewing each of his players as a blank slate, despite the fact that they were all seasoned pros. The first time Lombardi uttered this famous line, Green Bay Packer great Max McGee delivered his own immortal retort: "Uh, Coach, could you slow down a little? You're going too fast for us," and got a chuckle even from the unflappable Lombardi.

The contemporary business world has an expression for this mindset: "Assume nothing." The Zen Buddhists call it "beginner's mind." It's a mindset of humility and fresh inquiry, always looking for the most meaning and importance in the smallest things. I can't think of a better or more eloquent way of expressing it than, "Gentlemen, this is a football."

No matter how great your aspirations, how tall the dream and great the leap it means, the eternally repeating truth of the Slight Edge is that it is always built of small, simple steps. Easy to do— and just as easy not to do. Don't go too fast, and don't be too proud to stop, look at your life, and tell yourself, "This is a football."

To the coach, the football was the single step that begins the thousand-mile journey.

The football was Lombardi's penny.

Now it's time to find yours.

What one simple, single, easy-to-do activity can you do, day in and day out, that will have the greatest impact on your health; your personal development; your relationships; your finances; and your life itself?

In this next section, I'll ask you to walk yourself through these five areas of your life, one by one, to examine what they mean to you and where your dreams lie in each; and then lay out for yourself your dreams as goals (specific, vivid and with a timeline); the price you're willing to pay; a plan to start; and finally, one simple daily discipline that you will commit to doing each and every day from now on.

Go ahead, now, and take this stroll through your life; take a pencil as a walking stick.

The Slight Edge and Your Health

> Tell me what you eat and I will tell you what you are.
> — Jean Anthelme Brillat-Savarin

They say "the way to a man's heart is through his stomach." I don't know about that, but I do know this: that is the way to his destiny!

Health is one of the great riddles of existence. The foundational importance of everyday health is one of the most commonly known truths of human existence, and at the same time, it is also one of the most commonly and blatantly ignored. Everyone knows that "if you don't have your health, you have nothing." Our language is brimming over with related figures of speech:

At least you have your health.

You're only as old as you feel.

An ounce of prevention is worth a pound of cure.

Of the three "self-evident, inalienable rights" that ring from the American Declaration of Independence like a trumpet fanfare—"Life, Liberty and the pursuit of Happiness"—the first, without which the other two are irrelevant, is Life. And the most basic condition for the free, unencumbered experience of Life itself is health. There is nothing more basic than health—and there is no area of life where the Slight Edge is more vividly in operation, working either for you or against you.

That is perhaps your most important choice, day by day and hour by hour: whether to let your eating and physical activity build your fondest dreams—or dig your grave with your teeth. Hamlet wondered, "To be, or not to be?" You get to ask yourself that—and answer it—with every meal.

I always start with the area of health because when I'm in good physical shape I need less sleep, think more clearly, feel better about everything, and get more accomplished.

My simple daily discipline for my health is to exercise for at least half an hour.

When I started doing this, I have to admit, it didn't thrill me. That first day I went running was a real drag. I'd let myself go physically; it was harder than I'd expected it would be. That first day I ran for only about ten minutes; then over the next several weeks, I slowly worked my way up to my daily half hour. But even before that first week was over, I actually felt better than I had in months.

I usually say that the Slight Edge does not work quickly, but the truth is that often you'll get positive results fairly quickly. You may not achieve your ultimate goal in a week, a month or even a year or two, but you'll see the positive changes far sooner than you might expect. That's the way it was with my running.

I've said that successful people are willing to do those things unsuccessful people are not. And sometimes those things are uncomfortable. There is always a price you pay, and for me the price included my initial discomfort. But that price was quickly paid in full, and within weeks that discomfort faded. Now I'm uncomfortable when I *don't* run!

Those Slight Edge actions that are easy to do, and easy not to do? Soon, thanks to the powers of momentum, completion and habit, they become far easier to *do* than *not* to do!

Take a few moments to work out your own Slight Edge plan for your health. You don't need to feel limited or constricted by this exercise; you can always change and modify what you write here. Use a pencil! But do yourself a favor: don't skip over this and read on to the next. Actually, take the time to fill out each section, at least with some solid ideas to start with. You can always add to it and refine it later. In fact, you'll have to! That's how the Slight Edge works: you're not supposed to get it perfect the first time.

My dreams for my health (specific, vivid and with a timeline):

_____

_____

_____

_____

Price to pay:

_____

_____

_____

Plan to start:

_____

_____

_____

One simple daily discipline:

_____

_____

_____

The Slight Edge and Your Personal Development

> You will become as small as your controlling desire, or as great as your dominant aspiration.
> — James Allen, *As a Man Thinketh*

If you could wave a magic wand and have either a million dollars in the bank or a million-dollar mindset, which would you choose? I wouldn't hesitate for an instant: I'd rather be worth it than have it. Why? Because if I'm penniless but I have a million-dollar mindset, then it won't be long before I have the million dollars. But even if I don't have a million-dollar mindset, even with a cool million in the bank, it won't be long before I'm back to being penniless again!

Your income will never long exceed your own level of personal development. It may take a jump through happy circumstance or a lucky break—but if your own development does not quickly rise to meet that new level, it will quickly bounce back to the level where your personal development limits it, sure as if it were on a rubber band.

The same is true of your health; and of your relationships; and of your career; and of every aspect of your life. Over the long term, the limiting factor is never circumstance or fate; the limiting factor is always you. In the same way, and for the same reasons, the limitless scope of possibilities is also defined by one factor: you.

You already know of my passion for this area, and my number one Slight Edge recommendation. I teach everyone I work with to read at least ten pages of a powerful, life-transforming book each and every day. At the back of this book, I provide a list of some of my favorites; please add to it. Building your own personal self-improvement library may be the single most valuable and important investment (after your personal health) that you can make.

In addition to reading ten pages a day, I also teach people to listen to a self-improvement audiocassette or CD for at least fifteen minutes every day. The average person spends between 250 and 350 hours every year driving to and from this place and that. That's about forty minutes to an hour each and every day. If you spend that time listening to educational and self-improvement material, you'll have the equivalent of a Ph.D. on any subject you choose in just a few years. That's the Slight Edge.

When you're in your car, you can listen to music; but why build Garth Brooks' dream or Celine Dion's dream when you could by building your own? Listen to Jim Rohn's audiocassettes and CDs; he's a master at helping to build *your* dreams. Turn your car into a drive-time university! There are hundreds of powerful, masterful men and women to choose from. But you do have to make the choice.

I run with an iPod® and a headset, so I'm listening to audios while I run, which doubles my improvement. I travel quite a bit; when I do, I always pack my running shoes and iPod—so my Slight Edge half-hour run travels with me no matter where I go.

Because I double my time by listening to audios while I run, I also get to work directly on my personal development. Like health, this is a fundamental area for me, and is so powerful that it influences everything else going on in my life. When I first added the iPod to my daily run (in those days it was a Walkman), I started noticing positive changes in every other area of my life within the first couple of months.

Is it easy to do? Easy not to do? And if you don't do it, what will happen today? But that simple error in judgment, compounded over time, will leave you a willing participant in the conspiracy of mediocrity that nibbles away at the hopes, dreams and aspirations of the ninety-five percent who live out their days under the curse of Thoreau's famous epitaph for humanity (from *Walden*): "The mass of men lead lives of quiet desperation."

Listening to audios is an especially powerful Slight Edge tool because it can turn your "down time" into *up* time and double your productivity. You can drive to the store, or work or school; you can jog, roller-blade, bike or walk; sit on planes, stand in line, pedal, row, ski, stretch and lift weights—all the while feeding your mind through life-transforming audios.

And when you spend this time listening to true masters of the skills you seek to learn, you are using the third and most powerful method of learning: learning by modeling a mentor.

Take a few moments to work out your own Slight Edge plan for your personal development. Again, you needn't feel limited or constricted by this exercise; you can always change and modify what you write here. But don't skip on to the next: do yourself a favor and put down some initial thoughts. Use a pencil!

My dreams for my personal development (specific, vivid and with a timeline):

_____

_____

_____

_____

Price to pay:

_____

_____

_____

_____

Plan to start:

_____

_____

_____

_____

One simple daily discipline:

_____

_____

_____

_____

The Slight Edge and Your Relationships

> No man is an island, entire of itself; every man is a piece of the
> continent, a part of the main. If a clod be washed away by the
> sea, Europe is the less, as well as if promontory were, as well as
> if a manor of thy friend's or of thine own were. Any man's death
> diminishes me, because I am involved in mankind; and therefore
> never send to know for whom the bell tolls; it tolls for thee.
>
> — John Donne, *Devtions Upon Emergent Occasions*

One of the great ironic truths of human existence is that no matter how great our accomplishments, it is ultimately other people
who give it meaning. One reason that *Citizen Kane* continues to
rank among the greatest films ever made even today, more than
sixty years after it was made, is that it makes such a powerful statement of this truth: despite all his larger-than-life accomplishments, his millions, his international power as king-maker and
-breaker, in the final hour of his life, Charles Foster Kane was
consumed by a single thought: anguish over being ripped from his
childhood and thrust into the world alone at the age of eight. The
"great man" had no one to share his conquests and accomplishments with.

Earlier in this chapter, I wrote that the importance of health
is "one of the most commonly known truths of human existence—
and also one of the most commonly and blatantly ignored." The
same can be said for the importance of relationships. How often
have you heard of a successful businessperson who achieved great
financial success only at the expense of those two most precious
assets, good health and a rich family life?

When writing about the Law of Association, I mentioned the
importance of who you associate with in terms of its strategic
effect on you. But there is a greater truth about your associations,
too, because the relationships you choose are not only a means to
an end, they are also an end in themselves. All the success in the
world, as Charles Foster Kane learned, means little if there is no
one to share it with.

Relationships, too, are both built up and torn down in the
subtlest ways. Because most people are not aware of the Slight
Edge, the progress of their relationships tends to be a mystery.
What makes a marriage grow richer over the years for one couple,
and grow stale, empty and bitter for another? Nine times out of

ten—or better, nineteen times out of twenty—there is no single, significant answer. It is the little things, day by day, that add up over time to unshakable happiness or unsalvageable misery.

You've no doubt heard the expression, "It's the little things that count." There could scarcely be a more succinct statement of the Slight Edge—and chances are, you heard it said in the context of a relationship. The remembered birthdays, the little gifts, the gestures, the kind words, the remembered favorite color. The five minutes, snatched from an impossibly hectic day, to drop everything and hear the other's news. The word of encouragement; the reminder of your own belief in the other person. The listening.

It's been said that the most important statements of friendship are usually spoken with five words or less. That is the wisdom of the Slight Edge: those tiny thoughts and gestures that are startlingly easy to do ... and tragically easy not to do.

The future of every relationship you have, like that of your health, is a choice that is always in your hands, and it's no bigger than a penny. The key is to make the choice—and keep making it.

A special category of relationships, of course, is family. If you have children, you probably already know that they are in many ways your greatest legacy. No matter what the state of the educational system (and regardless of the decade or generation you're looking at, it always seems to be in a state of crisis!), the single most powerful influence on children will always be the people who raise them.

I have a daughter with unusually high self-esteem. This is no accident; in fact, it is a blessing I owe to the Slight Edge. When Amber was little, my wife and I knew that no matter how much we might want to, we could not change the 40,000 "No's" she was going to experience. That's what parents do: we set boundaries. The "No's" are something we do to protect our kids. That's our job.

We couldn't change the number of "No's"—but we could change the number of "Yes's." And that is exactly what we did.

One of the greatest gifts you can give your children is more "Yes's." So every time we said "No," we found a way also to say "Yes." By the time Amber went to school, she brought with her some 40,000 "No's," but she also brought with her something on the order of *160,000* "Yes's"—four times as much Yes as No. It changed her philosophy and her view of life. It changed her view of herself. As a result, it will change her entire life.

Though children are special, they are not unique in this respect: they are human beings, and so is everyone else. What kind of influence can you have on people simply by providing them with more "Yes's"? More influence than you can possibly imagine.

Toss a rock into a pond, and you'll see ripples from its impact spreading out until they reach the opposite shore. The same thing happens in life—only in most cases, you never see those ripples.

Everything you do is important. When you smile at a child and encourage him, or scold him and tell him he's no good—in either case, you may see the splash it makes, and you may see the first or second ripple, but the impact goes far, far beyond what you see. You don't see all the ripples.

You teach someone to read ten pages of a good book a day, and you may see how it changes her, but chances are you won't see how it changes her kids, and her kids' friends, and their friends, and their friends' kids ... And as these ripples spread out, they grow bigger! For better or for worse, with positive impact or negative impact, even your smallest actions create a ripple effect that has incalculably great impact on the world around you.

No doubt, you recognize this description of the "ripple effect"—it's our old friend, the Slight Edge.

Now, take a little time to think about the relationships in your life, and jot down a few thoughts about how you might work out your own Slight Edge plan for your deepening, strengthening and enriching those relationships. This is perhaps the most personal area of the five, and if you feel safer (since someone else might later be reading this copy of *The Slight Edge*), copy the worksheet below into a diary or journal, and fill in your answers there. Either way, do take the time to give it some thought and come up with your own answers. This is your life; this is the reason you're reading this book.

My dreams for my relationships (specific, vivid and with a time-line):

_____

_____

_____

_____

Price to pay:

_____

_____

_____

_____

Plan to start:

_____

_____

_____

_____

One simple daily discipline:

_____

_____

_____

_____

The Slight Edge and Your Finances

Winning is a habit. Unfortunately, so is losing.
— Vince Lombardi

It's no accident that our exploration of the Slight Edge began with the story of a penny doubled. The world of finances is one of the easiest places there is to see, objectively and logically, the power of the Slight Edge in action. Everyone knows about the power of compound interest, right?

Wrong. Everyone *thinks* they know about the power of compound interest; but most don't, not really. How many really do understand this power? Five percent ... the ones on the success curve side of the Slight Edge.

Remember the Pareto Principle as applied to your goals deadlines? "Eighty percent of everything you do tends to get done in the last twenty percent of the time available." There's a similar law at work in most people's finances, only it's worse. It's Parkinson's Law (coined by Prof. Cyril Northcote Parkinson): "Work expands to fill the time available for its completion." As applied to personal finances, it goes like this: *Whatever I have, I spend.* And for the last few generations, where easy-to-get consumer credit has flourished like weeds, it has come to be more like, *Whatever I have, I spend a little more!*

There is some good news here; in the last few years, the common sense of Slight Edge personal finances has started making a comeback. The 1998 book *The Millionaire Next Door* bucked the trend toward flashier, Donald Trump–style how-to finance books and instead gave example after example of how a cross-section of extraordinarily ordinary people became wealthy—without inheritance, without high-paying jobs, without making a killing in the stock market, without any of the usual "breakthrough" paths to riches, but by doing simple, easy things every day.

The first of its seven rules was, "Always live below your means." The book became a runaway best-seller.

When Stanley and Danko's book came out, my friends started reading it and calling me up, one by one, and saying, "Hey, Jeff, I just read this book, and it's about you!" For years, I kept our family living on $4,000 a month, no matter how much my income increased, and wouldn't let us raise that monthly threshold until I had a million (after taxes) in the bank. Then I raised it to $5,000! "Living below your means" is a classic Slight Edge strategy. David Bach's 2004 release, *The Automatic Millionaire*, continued in the same vein, and this book, along with his other titles (*Smart Women Finish Rich, Smart Couples Finish Rich* and *Start Late Finish Rich*), as well as his appearances on *The Oprah Winfrey Show*, have brought Bach's common-sense, Slight Edge financial advice into millions of households.

I'll bet you already have some very concrete thoughts about this area! Perhaps you've even been working this part out in the back of your mind ever since you read the story of the wealthy man and his two sons. Now's the time to start putting some of your thoughts to paper, and sketch out an initial plan for realizing your financial dreams and goals.

My dreams for my finances (specific, vivid and with a timeline):

_____

_____

_____

_____

Price to pay:

_____

_____

_____

_____

Plan to start:

_____

_____

_____

_____

One simple daily discipline:

_____

_____

_____

_____

The Slight Edge and Your Life!

There are only two paths in life. While we are traversing them, and especially in the earlier stages of the journey, they can often look alike, because appearances can be deceiving (and almost always are!). But they lead ultimately to very different places. One path leads to regret; the other leads to fulfillment.

In a typical goal-setting workshop, participants are often asked to set goals for a year ahead, five years, even ten years ahead. I went to a seminar once that had a unique approach: we were asked to set *one-hundred-year* goals!

What kind of goal would you set for one hundred years from now? What kind of impact can you imagine yourself having on the world that will last long after your own life has run its course? What will people remember you for after you have come and gone?

What impact do you wish to have on the world?

I used to ask people to think about their careers, their social and community activities, and their spiritual lives as distinct, different areas, much like their health and finances. I've come to look at this a little differently; I have realized that I would rather ask a larger question that embraces all these—career, social impact and spiritual life—as well as many others:

What do I want my life to mean?

This is the biggest area of all, because it includes all the others. Don't let its sheer size and scope intimidate you. After all, what we're looking for here is simple, little things you can do every day—things that are as easy to do, as they are not to do. The key here is not to spend too much time on this. Do the thing, and you shall have the power. Go ahead: take pencil in hand and sketch it out. Remember, it's your life; what would you like it to mean?

And remember this, too, no matter how lofty or long-term your life dreams may seem: "Gentlemen, this is a football." It starts with a penny. Start finding your pennies.

My dreams for my life (specific, vivid and with a timeline):

_____

_____

_____

_____

Price to pay:

_____

_____

_____

_____

Plan to start:

_____

_____

_____

_____

One simple daily discipline:

_____

_____

_____

_____

CHAPTER 12

It's a Wonderful Life

What do you want, Mary? Do you want the moon? If you want it,
I'll throw a lasso around it and pull it down for you. Hey. That's a
pretty good idea. I'll give you the moon ... then you can swallow
it, and it'll all dissolve, see ... and the moonbeams would shoot out
of your fingers and your toes and the ends of your hair ...
— George Bailey in *It's a Wonderful Life* (1946),
by Philip Van Doren Stern, Francis Goodrich,
Albert Hackett, and Frank Capra

The Beach Bum

You may be wondering what happened to Gorgeous George,
standing there in his cut-offs at the Orlando Country Club, gazing
at the rich and famous and happy and successful.

For whatever reason, as happens in so many people's lives, I
found myself staring squarely at a fork in the road, a point I now
refer to as a "day of disgust," that moment of impact we
sometimes hit in our lives when we face our circumstances and
make a decision to change.

In that instant, standing there sweating in the Florida heat, I
came to a moment of decision. I suddenly knew that I'd had it up
to here with where I was, what I was and who I was. Something
clicked; the tumblers in the lock fell into place; and I knew that I
could never go back to who I'd been only a minute earlier.

I knew that for things to change, *I* had to change. For things to get better, I had to get better.

I left the golf course.

I loaded my stereo and clothes into my 1964 Dodge Dart slant-six (all my possessions fit easily into the back seat with room for a passenger) and took off for home. It took me six days to get from Florida to Texas because the car kept overheating. It was the longest trip of my life.

The Super-Achiever

That semester, for the first time in my life, I got straight A's. I went on to business school and graduated at the very top of my class. Fresh out of college, I was recruited by Texas Instruments. I wanted to be in management, but they said, "If you want to be in management, you have to start in sales." Sales! I hated the idea of sales, knew nothing about it and was terrified of it, but sales it was. (And you already know what happened with that.) I worked at TI for five years and went to the very top levels of the company.

But corporate America wasn't for me. There was a lot of politics (which I hated) and it did not feel like I'd yet found the place where I belonged.

I went back to Albuquerque and started a solar energy company. I knew nothing about solar energy; I barely knew whether the sun came up in the east or in the west. But with four hundred solar companies in the state, New Mexico was the capital of the budding new industry, so ignorance or not, the smart course of action seemed clear.

And at first, it looked like I had indeed made the smart decision. Within two years, my company was in the top 20 and eventually we became the fifth largest solar energy company in America. I was thrilled. I was on top of the world. What I did not yet know was that nothing ever stays the same: everything is in motion. Everything changes.

Times changed. Tax laws changed. Our industry was hit hard. Before I knew what was happening, I had lost everything, gone back to zero and below—owing more money than I thought I could ever even hope to make again.

The Lesson

The night my car was towed away, I sat in despair and thought: *This just isn't fair. After living as a failure all my life, I woke up one day and came to my senses, went back to college, applied myself like crazy, entered at the bottom and graduated at the top, worked for a major corporation for five years and went to the very top, built my own company in less than five years and went to the top ... and here I am, after twelve long years of building toward success, at the bottom again! I'm more broke today than when I was Gorgeous George on the beach!*

Twelve years of blood and guts, and I was more of a failure than ever. I couldn't wrap my head around it. I couldn't see the logic, the justice, the reasons for any of it. Was life just inherently unfair? Was that it? Was there simply no rhyme or reason for anything? Was there no point in even trying?

That was when I began to examine more carefully what had happened in my life.

I had been a college dropout, a beach bum and a complete financial failure. And I had also been a straight-A student, a top corporate salesperson, a super-achieving entrepreneur in a cutting-edge industry and a complete financial success. And all of those had been the same person. So what was the difference? It made no sense.

Or did it?

For the first time, I began to see that over the years of my roller-coaster career, I had gone through a rich sequence of experiences that held the secrets to success as well as to failure. I had proven to myself, beyond any shadow of doubt, the depths of failure that simple daily errors in judgment could produce. I had also seen what simple daily disciplines could accomplish. I just hadn't quite realized what I knew.

It was time to pull away the veil of circumstance and look right at the heart of the matter. To go behind the results and examine the actions, and behind the actions to find the attitudes, and behind the attitudes to discover the thinking that held them there.

That was when I began to discover and explore the Slight Edge.

Since that time, I have built some extraordinary businesses and earned more money than I ever dreamed of back when I was a corporate salesperson or solar energy entrepreneur. I've also experienced more joy and fulfillment within my family and other relationships than I knew was possible. I've also discovered new vistas in my own investment in my own development, in terms of both health and learning.

Perhaps most important than all of that is that I've built a philosophy that is grounded in reality, in the way things actually work—not on luck and the mystery of the quantum leap, but on the power of the water hyacinth.

I could lose it all tomorrow. (It's happened before; I'd survive.) But there is something I cannot lose, and with that one thing I could start from scratch, with a penny, and build it all back up again. That one thing is the Slight Edge.

Where to Go from Here

Some day, when I have the time, I'm going to ... Some day, when I have the money, I'm going to ...

Have you ever said that? *"Some day ... "* It's a way we have of reinforcing the illusion that the future is safely far removed, that it doesn't really touch us. It's a lie. Not an intentional, willful deception, but a lie nonetheless.

Let's say that, "some day," I'm going to travel around the world. If that's really true, if I absolutely intend for that to happen, then I'm making plans. If it's not practical today for me to just up and circumnavigate, I can look at what needs to happen first, and second, and third, to end up with that result.

When I set that process in motion, the words "some day ... " disappear. I'm making it happen today, *right now*. In a very real sense, I am *already taking* the trip. It may be three years before we actually take the trip, but the words "some day ... " no longer apply, so I stop using them.

When I say "some day ... " I'm not really talking about the future. The future is a reality that I'm connected to by what I'm doing *right now*. "Some day ... " is about some vague possibility that I'm not taking seriously.

"Some day ... " is not a vision of my future. "Some day ... " is a fantasy—nothing more.

Here's the damage we do with this illusion. We give weight to our "some day ... " fantasies; we squeeze some sense of enjoyment from them as if they were real—and thereby give ourselves permission to take *no practical action* whatsoever while we swim in the comforting sense that those some-day scenarios will move closer to the unfolding present on their own.

They won't. The wistful, wouldn't-it-be-nice pretendings of maybe-futures do not insert themselves into your reality of their own accord. You've got to go claim them. Ask yourself: "What is there in my life that I hold as 'Some day ... '?"

Some day ... The eighth day of the week. The only day that never comes.

This is the day—this one. Right here. Right now.

— John David Mann, *The Eighth Day of the Week*

Abraham Lincoln spoke about taking twice as long to sharpen the axe as to hack at the tree. In your life, you are the axe; the Slight Edge is how you sharpen it. Sharpen yourself and pursue your path through those simple, small, easy disciplines, and compounded over time, they will take you to the top.

Do one simple, daily discipline in each of these five key areas of your life—your health, your personal development, your relationships (which includes family), your finances, and your life overall (which includes the meaning and purpose of your life)— that forwards your success in each of those areas ...

Make a habit of doing some sort of daily review of these Slight Edge activities, either through keeping a journal, a list, working with a Slight Edge buddy, a coach, or some other regular, consistent means ...

Spend high-quality time with men and women who have achieved goals and dreams similar to yours; in other words, model successful mentors, teachers, gurus, masters and allies, and do it daily, weekly and monthly ...

... and you will find yourself on the success curve—and you *will* turn your dreams into realities.

Successful people do what unsuccessful people are not willing to do; they put the Slight Edge to work for them, rather than against them, every day. They refuse to let themselves be swayed by their feelings, moods or attitudes; they rule their lives by their philosophies, and do what it takes to get the job done, whether they feel like it or not.

Successful people don't look for shortcuts, nor do they hope for the "big breakthrough." They are always open to quantum leaps, knowing that such opportune moments do present themselves from time to time, but they focus on sticking to their knitting and doing what they've put in front of themselves to do. They step onto the path of mastery and once having set foot there, they stay on that path throughout their lives.

Successful people never blame circumstances or other people; instead, they take full responsibility for their lives. They use the past as a lesson but do not dwell in it, and instead, let themselves be pulled up and forward by the compelling force of the future. They know that the path that leads to the success curve and the one that leads to the failure curve are only a hair's breadth apart, separated only by the distinction of simple, "insignificant" actions that are just as easy not to do as they are to do—and that this difference will ultimately make all the difference.

Successful people know how to use the natural tension to close the gap from point A, where they are, to point B, where they want to be. They understand why the tortoise won the race; they know that "steady wins the race," and that the Slight Edge is the optimal rate of growth for them.

Successful people use inertia to build momentum, making their upward journey of success easier and easier. They know how to identify habits that don't serve them and replace them with those that do. They understand the powers of reflection, completion and celebration and they harness them constantly, using their radar for unfinished business to propel them forward rather than being sucked backward and downward.

Successful people acquire the three kinds of knowledge they need to succeed. They create an ongoing support system of both book smarts and street smarts, learning through study and through doing, and they catalyze and accelerate that knowledge by finding mentors and modeling their successful behavior. They plan, they do, and then they review, again and again and again.

Successful people are always asking: "Who am I spending time with? Are they the people who best represent where I want to be headed?" They form powerful relationships with positive people; they carefully build Mastermind groups, work with those groups regularly and take them seriously; and they do not hesitate to disassociate themselves, when necessary, from people who are consistently negative and threaten to drag them down.

Successful people read at least ten pages of a powerful, life-transforming book each day, and listen to at least fifteen minutes of educational and inspirational audiotapes and CDs every day.

Successful people go to work on their philosophy first, because they know it is the source of their attitudes, actions, results and the quality of their lives.

They understand that they can increase their success by *doubling their rate of failure.*

They understand activity and because they *do the thing*, they *have the power.*

They understand the power of simple things.

They understand the power of daily disciplines.

They understand the power of the water hyacinth, and know how to use it.

They know how to keep paddling when others give up and sink.

They know when they are being offered the choice of wisdom.

Successful people understand the Slight Edge, and they put it to work for them.

So ... where do you go from here? Find your penny—then start doubling it.

Life-Transforming Resources

As a Man Thinketh, James Allen
Multiple Streams of Income, Robert G. Allen
Smart Women Finish Rich, David Bach
The Automatic Millionaire, David Bach
Start Late, Finish Rich, David Bach
The One Minute Manager, Ken Blanchard and Spencer Johnson
Mach II with Your Hair on Fire, Richard B. Brooke
The Aladdin Factor, Jack Canfield and Mark Victor Hansen
Dare to Win, Jack Canfield and Mark Victor Hansen
How to Win Friends and Influence People, Dale Carnegie
Acres of Diamonds, Russell H. Conwell
The Richest Man in Babylon, George S. Clason
The 7 Habits of Highly Effective People, Stephen R. Covey
The 8th Habit: From Effectiveness to Greatness, Stephen R. Covey
Think and Grow Rich, Napoleon Hill
Rich Dad Poor Dad, Robert T. Kiyosaki and Sharon L. Lechter
Cashflow Quadrant: Rich Dad's Guide to Financial Freedom,
    Robert T. Kiyosaki and Sharon L. Lechter
Conversations with Millionaires, Mike Litman, Jason Oman, et al.
The Greatest Salesman in the World, Og Mandino
The 21 Irrefutable Laws of Leadership, John C. Maxwell
Failing Forward, John C. Maxwell
The Power of Positive Thinking, Norman Vincent Peale
You Can If You Think You Can, Dr. Norman Vincent Peale
You Were Born Rich, Bob Proctor

Leadership Secrets of Attila the Hun, Wess Roberts
Cultivating an Unshakable Character, Jim Rohn
Seven Strategies for Wealth and Happiness, Jim Rohn
The Art of Exceptional Living, Jim Rohn
The Challenge to Succeed, Jim Rohn
The Five Major Pieces to the Life Puzzle, Jim Rohn
The Seasons of Life, Jim Rohn
True Leadership, Jan Ruhe, Art Burleigh, et al.
The Magic of Thinking Big, David Schwartz
The Millionaire Next Door,
    Thomas J. Stanley and William D. Danko
21 Success Secrets of Self-Made Millionaires, Brian Tracy
The Science of Getting Rich, Wallace D. Wattles
All You Can Is All You Can Do, But All You Can Do Is Enough,
    Art Williams
Breaking the Rules, Kurt Wright

Many of these books are also available on audiocassette and/or CD.

About the Author

JEFF OLSON has spoken to more than a thousand audiences throughout the United States and around the world. Over the past twenty years, he has helped hundreds of thousands of individuals achieve better levels of financial freedom and personal excellence.

Born and raised in Albuquerque, New Mexico, Jeff took his undergraduate degree in marketing from the University of New Mexico, graduating at the top of his class. While in graduate school, he was hired by the Albuquerque Airport as one of the youngest airport managers in the industry. He then went to work for Texas Instruments, where he worked his way through its sales ranks to become an intelligence systems manager in less then five years. He left TI to form Sun Aire of America, a company devoted to all aspects of solar energy, from design and manufacturing to marketing and distribution. While with Sun Aire Jeff acquired an exhaustive "street smarts" education in every aspect of sales, marketing and distribution, and within four years Sun Aire was one of the largest solar companies in the United States.

Since his experiences with TI and Sun Aire, Jeff has worked with a series of sales, marketing and distribution companies, building three different sales and distribution forces from scratch to multimillion-dollar organizations. In the early '90s, he put in place a national satellite-training program for an independent sales force by placing 30,000 individual satellite dishes in homes across the country. Based on that experience, he went on to form TPN, a company that became one of the largest personal development training companies in the nation. Through TPN Jeff worked with such *New York Times* best-selling authors and legendary figures of personal development as Tony Alessandra, Les Brown, Nido Qubein, Jim Rohn, Brian Tracy and many others, producing more than 900 television programs with them and presenting seminars in every major city in the United States.

Jeff describes himself as "a perpetual student of personal development," and he is as devoted to health and fitness as he is to personal and financial success. Jeff currently divides his time between his homes in Dallas, Texas, and Fort Lauderdale, Florida.